Born Global Firms

Born Global Firms

A New International Enterprise

S. Tamer Cavusgil
Georgia State University

Gary Knight
Florida State University

business**expert**
Press

First published in 2009 by
Business Expert Press, LLC
222 East 46th Street, New York, NY 10017
www.businessexpertpress.com

ISBN-13: 978-1-60649-012-9 (paperback)
ISBN-10: 1-60649-012-5 (paperback)

ISBN-13: 978-1-60649-013-6 (e-book)
ISBN-10: 1-60649-013-3 (e-book)

DOI 10.4128/9781606490136

A publication in the Business Expert Press International Business
collection

Collection ISSN: 1948-2752 (print)
Collection ISSN: 1948-2760 (electronic)

Cover design by Artistic Group—Monroe, NY
Interior design by Scribe, Inc.

First edition: June 2009

10 9 8 7 6 5 4 3 2 1

Printed in the United States of America.

Abstract

This book describes companies that conduct international business at or near the founding of the firm. Despite the limited resources that usually characterize new businesses, these "Born Global" firms achieve substantial international sales from an early stage in their development. They internationalize rapidly—the period from domestic establishment to initial foreign market entry is often three or fewer years. Born globals are emerging in sizable numbers worldwide. Until recently, international business was mainly the domain of large, well-resourced multinational enterprises (MNEs). The appearance of large numbers of born global firms is revolutionizing the traditional character of international business and helping reshape the global economy. This book helps managers and scholars understand the born global phenomenon. We offer a comprehensive treatment of born globals, from distinctive features of these companies, to strategies that they use for international success, to implications of the phenomenon for international small- and medium-sized enterprises. We review useful theories and frameworks and introduce a new field based on the born global phenomenon—international entrepreneurship. We provide a comprehensive literature review and an explanation of major theories that explain the born global firm. This complete guide to born global firms was written by leading experts in the field.

Specifically, we report on

- the existence of born global firms around the world;
- case studies of born global firms;
- born globals as international small- and medium-sized enterprises;
- facilitating factors in the emergence of born global firms;
- a literature review and key theories on born global firms for scholars;
- how the born global phenomenon challenges traditional internationalization theories;
- the critical role of entrepreneurial orientation in the emergence of born globals;
- implications for managers of born globals and other small, internationalizing firms; and
- how born globals point to the future of international trade.

Keywords

born global firms; born globals; born global; international entrepreneurship; early internationalization; rapid internationalization; international strategy; international business; international trade; international small- and medium-sized enterprises; international entrepreneurial orientation; international SME

Contents

Introduction

The born global firm is defined as "a business organization that, from inception, seeks to derive significant competitive advantage from the use of resources and the sale of outputs in multiple countries" (Oviatt & McDougall, 1994, p. 49). In due course, these distinctive firms are gradually becoming the norm among companies that do international business. The distinguishing feature of born global firms is that their origins are international, as demonstrated by management's global focus and the commitment of certain types of resources to international activities. Here we emphasize not the size but rather the age by which the firm ventures into foreign markets. In contrast to the traditional pattern of businesses that operate in the home country for many years and gradually evolve into international trade, born globals begin with a "borderless" view of the world and develop the strategies needed to expand abroad at or near the firm's founding. The focus is on the phenomenon of early internationalization and the approaches that companies leverage for achieving superior performance in international business from the inception of the firm.

In this book, we aim to make several contributions. First, we undertake a comprehensive investigation of a unique breed of international organization, the born global firm. Second, in the process of describing born globals, we highlight the importance of key organizational elements that engender international success in born globals and small internationalizing firms in general. We highlight the need to understand the interaction between organizational orientations and strategies. Third, we also examine the linkage between key orientations and strategies and international performance in born global firms.

Specifically, in chapter 1 we introduce born global firms and present evidence on how they are emerging in large numbers worldwide. We summarize conditions for, and distinctive features of, born globals and describe factors that help explain why such firms internationalize early. We also discuss born globals as a distinctive category of international small and medium-sized enterprise.

In chapter 2, we describe factors that facilitate the emergence of born global firms. The most important of these factors are globalization and technological advances. We discuss the implications of these trends.

In chapter 3, we summarize major extant literature on born global firms. The literature review is partly intended to support scholars in conducting research.

In chapter 4, we summarize major theoretical explanations and frameworks on born globals. We also discuss how the born global phenomenon might challenge traditional views on the internationalization of the firm. Next, we review major orientations and strategies associated with born global firms, particularly as these relate to their performance in international business. In addition to aiding scholars, the chapter is intended to guide managers and others in how to make born globals and international small and medium-sized firms succeed.

In chapter 5, we introduce the field of "international entrepreneurship," which describes the process of creatively discovering and exploiting opportunities that lie outside a firm's domestic markets in the pursuit of competitive advantages. The new field offers rich opportunities to employ and integrate perspectives that enrich knowledge development on born globals. In this chapter, we also highlight the critical role of entrepreneurial orientation in early internationalizing firms.

We devote chapter 6 to describing the implications for company managers and how they might devise strategies and other approaches to ensuring international business success. Given that born globals succeed despite scarce resources and other organizational shortcomings, even managers of large established companies can learn much from the success of these remarkable young firms.

In chapter 7, we highlight how born global firms in many ways represent the future of international business. We also lay out future research directions, to aid scholars and students in conducting research on born global firms. We close the chapter by discussing practical considerations for scholars conducting research on born globals.

In appendix A, we summarize case studies on numerous born global firms. In appendix B, we outline a method for developing an international business plan that can be used by managers in new or young companies seeking to become born global firms.

This book describes the emergence of a distinct breed of international firm, more capable than ever of succeeding in foreign markets via the application of a specific constellation of orientations and strategies. Born global firms herald a new era of enormous benefits that will flow from ideas, goods, and people as countless small firms trade with each other around a world that is becoming an economic global village.

CHAPTER 1

Born Global Firms:
An Introduction

History and Heraldry is a company in England that specializes in gifts for history buffs and those with English ancestry. Within a few years after the firm's founding, History and Heraldry was selling its products in 60 countries, with exports generating about 70% of total production. The firm's biggest markets include France, Germany, Italy, Spain, and the United States (Coleman, 2005). Cosmos Corporation, Inc., is a young company in the United States that makes binoculars, telescopes, and various other optical devices. Within a few years of its founding, Cosmos began selling its products in Europe and Japan. Soon after that, the firm had expanded its sales to some 28 countries around the world.

This book describes companies that conduct international business at or near their founding. International business refers to the performance of trade and investment activities by companies across national borders. When they engage in international business, companies organize, source, manufacture, market, and generally conduct value-adding activities in two or more countries. Companies have engaged in international business throughout history. In the modern era, countless firms operate in multiple countries and undertake a variety of international trade and investment activities. Companies seek customers and engage in collaborative relationships with foreign business partners. They leverage foreign sites to produce products and services. They seek comparative advantages by seeking a wide range of resources located around the world.

Since the early 1980s, international business has gained speed and complexity. It is facilitated by the globalization of markets, modern information and communications technologies, and globe-spanning transportation systems that have made conducting international business easier for all firms.

Companies seek international market opportunities today more than ever before, touching the lives of billions of people around the world.

Much of this activity has been stimulated by "globalization," the growing economic integration and interdependency of countries worldwide. Globalization has coincided with massive growth in international transactions. For example, in 1960 international trade worldwide was modest—about $100 billion per year. Today it accounts for a huge proportion of the world economy, amounting to over $10 trillion annually. There are more opportunities to market products internationally than ever before.

Going international has also gotten easier. A few decades ago, international business was dominated by large, multinational companies. Today, largely thanks to various facilitating factors, companies of all sizes regularly market their offerings around the world. The number of firms doing international business has grown enormously.

Companies undertake international business for a variety of reasons, including the ability to

- seek growth via market diversification,
- earn higher profits from lucrative foreign markets,
- better serve existing customers who have located abroad,
- gain economies of scale in production and marketing,
- amortize the costs of product development and marketing across many markets,
- obtain new product ideas from foreign settings, and
- confront competitors more effectively in competitors' home markets.

Historically, the most popular markets for international business were advanced-economy countries in North America and Europe, as well as Australia, New Zealand, and Japan. Today firms increasingly target "emerging markets," such as Brazil, China, India, Mexico, and Saudi Arabia. There are substantial market opportunities even in developing economies in Africa, Latin America, and Southeast Asia. The attractiveness of emerging markets arises primarily from growing affluence in these countries.

Within this contemporary environment, companies that conduct international business at or near their founding are emerging in sizable numbers worldwide. Despite the scarce financial, human, and tangible resources that characterize most new businesses, most born global firms achieve considerable success in international business early in their development. They progress from one stage of internationalization to the next relatively rapidly. For example, the period from establishing the firm to initial foreign market entry is often three or fewer years (Autio, Sapienza, & Almeida, 2000; McDougall & Oviatt, 2000; OECD, 1997; Rennie, 1993). Born globals achieve substantial international sales from an early stage, selling a wide range of products and services in markets around the world.

In this book, we employ the term *born global* to describe such companies (McKinsey, 1994; Rennie, 1993). In recent decades, various trends have converged that encourage the emergence of this relatively new class of global firm. In the international business literature, born globals have been called "global start-ups" (e.g., Oviatt & McDougall, 1995), "instant internationals" (e.g., Fillis, 2001), and "international new ventures" (e.g., Oviatt & McDougall, 1994). The term born global was originally used by McKinsey & Co. (1993) to describe early internationalizing firms in Australia. In reality, few of the companies were "global" from inception— most internationalized within one or two years of their founding. Born global, however, is a descriptive term and we will use it throughout this book. These companies are leading exemplars of successful international small and medium-sized enterprises (SMEs, which we define in this book as firms with 500 or fewer employees). Born globals have been observed and described in virtually all major trading countries (e.g., OECD, 1997), across industry sectors (e.g., Knight & Cavusgil, 2004), and in both high- and low-tech industries (e.g., Madsen & Servais, 1997; Rennie, 1993).

Historically, in most countries, international business was the domain of large multinational enterprises (MNEs). Companies such as IBM, Siemens, and Toyota have existed for many decades and employ thousands of employees who established subsidiaries and affiliates in nations around the world. In recent years, however, trends such as globalization and the appearance of various technologies have facilitated the emergence of born global firms. The appearance of large numbers of born globals is revolutionizing the traditional character of international business, and helping to reshape the global economy. The box presents an extended example of a typical born global firm.

An Example: Vellus Products, Inc.

Vellus is a small company based in the United States that makes customized shampoos, conditioners, sprays, and accessories for grooming pets. Vellus started doing international business within a few years of its founding in order to increase sales and diversify its customer base (Judy, 1998; Pavilkey, 2001). The firm sells its products in numerous countries, including grooming aids formulated for the distinctive skin and hair of dogs and horses. For example, stable owners in the United Arab Emirates regularly buy Vellus horse grooming products. Vellus's first foreign sale was to a Taiwanese importer who purchased $25,000 worth of product to sell at Taiwan dog shows. As word spread about the uniqueness and superior quality of Vellus's offerings, the firm expanded into multiple country markets. Vellus leverages the support of distributors and other intermediaries abroad. Vellus's management attends trade fairs in target markets to find customers and sign up distributors.

Vellus's management does regular market research to learn how to do business abroad. Managers had to adapt the firm's marketing and other activities to meet conditions in various markets. In England, for example, dog show exhibitors prefer pooches with modest topknots, while those in the United States prefer exotic hair styles. In England, dog exhibitors prefer shih tzus with a big head that are somewhat lower to the ground, while U.S. exhibitors prefer more leg and a shorter back. These preferences determine the types of brushes and shampoos that each country needs. Today, Vellus sells its products in over 28 countries. Roughly half the firm's revenues come from international sales.

Born global firms can be found in advanced economies—such as Australia, Denmark, Japan, and the United States—and in emerging markets—such as China and India. While born globals have always existed, especially in countries with small domestic markets, such businesses are now appearing in markedly large numbers around the world. The upswing in the emergence of born globals began to be reported in the popular press in the late 1980s and early 1990s (e.g., Luostarinen et al., 1994; Nakamura, 1992; Rennie, 1993; *Wall Street Journal*, 1989). Pioneering global start-ups account for a substantial portion of growth in national merchandise exports in many countries (e.g., *Economist*, 1993; Luostarinen et al., 1994; McKinsey & Co., 1993; OECD, 1997). The born global phenomenon is occurring literally throughout the world in a wide range of business environments and industries (e.g., Nikkei Sangyoo Shimbun, 1995; OECD, 1997; Simon, 1996).

In the business academic field, the born global phenomenon has been investigated in the management literature (e.g., Knight & Cavusgil, 1997; Oviatt & McDougall, 1994), in the business and textbook press (e.g., Cavusgil, Knight, & Riesenberger, 2008; Nikkei Sangyoo Shimbun, 1995), by leading business consulting firms (e.g., McKinsey & Co., 1993; Rennie, 1993), and by the OECD and United Nations (e.g., 1993). These developments underscore how born globals have assumed greater prominence and become a distinctive category of enterprise in the world economy.

Born globals have various characteristics, summarized in Exhibit 1.1. These firms exist in most industries and tend to be formed by entrepreneurs with a strong international outlook. Managers tend to see the world as their marketplace, often emphasizing strong international marketing skills. To the extent this breed of enterprise can be an engine of growth for global product-market innovations and economic development, the emergence of born global firms is an important trend.

Historically, it was believed that companies had to build a strong domestic base before venturing into foreign markets. One reason was the high fixed costs of entering a new market at a distance, including the costs of gaining market information and of managing agents or representatives to establish effective sales organizations. However, dramatic changes in recent years are facilitating the ability of companies to compete in international business from the earliest days after the founding of the firm.

Distinctive Features Of Born Global Firms

As represented in Exhibit 1.1, born global firms typically possess the following characteristics:

Highly active in international markets from or near founding. Most born globals rely on exporting as their main foreign market entry mode (e.g.,

Exhibit 1.1. Conditions for, and Distinctive Features of, Born Global Firms

Facilitating Factors:

- Globalization of markets
- Advances in communications and information technologies
- Advances in production technologies
- Global niche markets
- Global networks

Distinctive Features of Born Global Firms:

- Highly active in international markets from or near founding
- Characterized by limited financial and tangible resources
- Found across most industries
- Managers have a strong international outlook and international entrepreneurial orientation
- Often emphasize differentiation strategy
- Often emphasize superior product quality
- Leverage advanced communications and information technologies
- Typically use external, independent intermediaries for distribution in foreign markets

Internationalization Triggers:

- Export pull
- Export push
- Worldwide monopoly position
- Product-market conditions necessitating international involvement
- Superior product offerings
- Global network relationships
- Global niche markets

OECD, 1997). Born globals begin exporting their products or services within a couple of years after their founding and may export a quarter or more of their total production. Most advance through subsequent stages of internationalization, collaboration with foreign partners, and even undertaking of foreign direct investment. Many born globals operate in dozens of countries throughout the world.

Characterized by limited financial and tangible resources. Given their youth, born globals tend to be relatively small firms. Most are SMEs. Being smaller organizations, born globals have far fewer financial, human, and tangible resources than the large MNEs that have long been the dominant force in global trade and investment. Historically, international business was beyond the reach of most smaller firms. However, various trends have made doing international business a viable option for all firms. As a result, companies that internationalize at or near their founding—born globals— have been emerging in substantial numbers worldwide.

Found across most industries. Some scholars believe that the born global phenomenon is concentrated in high-technology industries. However, there is substantial evidence to suggest that the phenomenon is more widespread (e.g., Moen, 2002; Rennie, 1993). For example, in Denmark, the breadth of represented sectors is far greater, including such industries as metal fabrication, furniture, processed food, and consumer products (Madsen & Servais, 1997).

Managers have a strong international outlook and international entrepreneurial orientation. Top management in born globals tend to view the world as their marketplace from the outset of the firm's founding. Unlike many traditional companies, managers typically do not see foreign markets as simple adjuncts to the domestic market. Many born globals are formed by proactive managers with a strongly entrepreneurial mindset. An entrepreneurial orientation reflects substantial proactiveness and aggressiveness in the pursuit of international markets. It is associated with managerial vision, proclivity for risk taking, and proactive competitive posture. Entrepreneurial orientation can also denote a propensity to innovation, which reflects the firm's tendency to pursue new ideas and develop new products and services.

Often emphasize differentiation strategy. Born globals tend to emphasize differentiation strategy (Porter, 1980), which implies offering distinctive products of differentiated design. Many born globals target relatively distinctive products to niche markets that may be too small to interest large firms. When using differentiation strategy, the firm stimulates customer loyalty by uniquely meeting a particular need. Differentiation strategy may be especially appropriate for born globals because their resources are relatively specialized and they typically target niche markets. People and firms increasingly demand specialized and customized products, and niche markets have become an important source of opportunities for small firms.

Often emphasize superior product quality. Many born globals offer state-of-the-art products that are better designed and higher quality than competitors' offerings. Born globals are often at the leading technological edge of their industry or product category. Technological prowess confers significant advantages for pursuing markets around the world. Such firms do not usually operate in "commodity" markets. Rather, they are likely to target niche markets, to which they offer superior quality products. In fact, the founding of born globals is often associated with the development of new products or services.

Leverage advanced communications and information technologies. Information and communications technologies allow smaller firms to process information efficiently and communicate with partners and customers worldwide at practically zero cost. Advances in communications have practically eliminated boundaries between firms and help companies of any size manage business systems spread all around the world. Many born globals leverage the technologies to segment customers into narrow global market niches and skillfully serve highly specialized buyer needs.

Typically use external, independent intermediaries for distribution in foreign markets. Given their smaller size and limited resources, most born globals expand internationally via exporting (e.g., OECD, 1997). Thus, they engage in direct international sales or leverage the resources of independent intermediaries located abroad. Many born globals rely on external facilitators, such as FedEx and DHL, to organize international shipments. Exporting and leveraging independent intermediaries helps make born global international operations "flexible." This means firms can enter or withdraw from foreign markets relatively quickly and easily. More experienced born globals export in combination with other strategies, such as joint ventures and foreign direct investment. The low-cost, low-risk nature of exporting, combined with the ability to leverage foreign partners, makes exporting especially suitable for young companies.

Evidence On Born Global Firms

Since the widespread appearance of born globals, numerous scholars have sought to shed light on this fascinating phenomenon. Research suggests that born globals are emerging throughout the world (e.g., Chuushoo Kigyoo Cho, 1995; McKinsey & Co., 1993; OECD, 1997; United Nations, 1993). In Australia, for example, some 25% of newly emerging exporters are born global, sometimes exporting more than three-quarters of their total production (e.g., McKinsey & Co., 1993). The box highlights the findings of Rennie's study of born global firms in Australia (1993). A comprehensive study of manufacturers in Europe revealed that more than half were global start-ups (Madsen & Servais, 1997). Simon (1996) investigated 500 "hidden champions," highly successful international niche players from Europe and North America, and found that more than one-third had begun to sell their products in foreign markets in their first year of business. The Japanese have reported in various publications on the widespread emergence of born globals (e.g., Chuushoo Kigyoo Cho, 1995; Nikkei Sangyoo Shimbun, 1995). In Taiwan, Chang and Grub (1992) described how most of the companies in their sample of firms in the information technology industry had expanded abroad by pursuing narrow market niches. The Taiwanese firms began selling to foreign markets shortly after their founding to target markets as diverse as Spain, Scandinavia, and the former Soviet Union.

In our research on born globals in Europe, we found that such companies often are less "global" than comparable firms in the United States (Knight, Madsen, & Servais, 2004). For example, born globals in Denmark often confine themselves to other countries in the European Union. Many of these firms are *regionally* based, while their competitors in Japan and the United States often build up substantial *global* operations. As the feasibility of protecting their competitiveness and regional performance is eroded by economic integration and worldwide globalization, the competitive position of regionally based firms can deteriorate over time. In order to

Born Global Firms in Australia

The term "born global" was coined by Michael Rennie in an article written in the *McKinsey Quarterly* (1993). Rennie described "a new breed of [firm that] shows that it is possible to succeed in world markets without an established domestic base." Rennie investigated the rise of numerous young SMEs in Australia that successfully compete against large, established players in global markets. The young firms did not slowly build their way into international business; rather, they internationalized at or near their founding. Rennie cited the example of Cochlear, a $40 million (annual sales) firm that generated 95% of its sales from abroad. Cochlear specializes in high-tech ear implants for the deaf. The firm owes much of its success to strong links with hospitals and research units around the world, as well as collaborative research with a network of institutions worldwide.

In his study of 300 firms, Rennie (1993) found that Australian born globals began exporting, on average, only two years after founding and obtained about three-quarters of their revenues from export sales. Despite their small size (total average sales of $16 million), the firms successfully competed against larger established players worldwide. Born globals represent about 20% of Australia's high-value-added manufacturing exports. Rennie (1993) argued that the emergence of born globals reveals how SMEs can power a nation's economic growth. He noted that born globals account for a growing share of exports in other countries as well.

reap all the benefits of the global marketplace, some European born globals are expanding their international reach to markets outside Europe.

Born Globals as International Small- and Medium-Sized Enterprises

Born globals are a type of small and medium-sized enterprise (SME). Usually classified as firms with 500 or fewer employees, SMEs make up over 95% of all companies and create about 50% of value added worldwide (OECD, 1997). In a study of 18 countries, the Organisation for

Economic Cooperation and Development (OECD) reported that international SMEs now make up a very substantial contribution to the world economy. SMEs account for more than one-third of world manufactured exports, and over one million of these firms are very active in international trade (OECD, 1997). In fact, SMEs now comprise the majority of firms doing international business. Many of these SMEs are born globals. Most are young firms that are internationalizing earlier than ever before.

In the United States, SMEs account for a great proportion of all U.S. exporters. From 1992 to 2004, they represented nearly 100% of the growth in the U.S. exporter population, swelling from about 108,000 firms in 1992 to over 225,000 firms by 2004. SMEs were responsible for nearly a third of merchandise exports from the United States in 2006. A great proportion were wholesalers, distributors, and other nonmanufacturing firms (Neupert, Baughn, & Dao, 2006; World Bank, 2005).

SMEs are more active in international business than ever before (e.g., OECD, 1997). They are often the backbone for entrepreneurship and innovation in national economies. In Eastern Europe, the development of emerging market countries is driven increasingly by the rise of small and midsize fast-growth firms. These firms range from Latvian coffee shop chain Double Coffee to Hungarian employment recruiter CVO Group. Many of Eastern Europe's small firms are not in manufacturing, but in intellectual, knowledge-intensive industries, such as software and consulting (Matlack, 2006).

In recent years, the national governments of Australia, Britain, Canada, China, New Zealand, and the United States have undertaken aggressive campaigns to help more SMEs become exporters. Governments sponsor trade fairs and trade missions that connect SMEs with distributors and other facilitators in promising foreign markets. The World Bank assists SME exporters from emerging markets by increasing access to capital and developing their international business skills. While most SMEs export to advanced economies, an increasing number target emerging markets, such as China and Mexico.

For example, Pharmed Group, based in Florida, is a full-line distributor of medical, surgical, and pharmaceutical supplies. Hoping to expand export sales, the firm signed a deal with Drogao, a major drug store chain in Brazil. Export sales have contributed significantly to Pharmed's growth. Another

SME, Optical Xport, exports optical lenses and frames to customers in West and Central Africa from its low-cost manufacturing base in Senegal. These efforts increase the flow of medical supplies and eyeglasses to the poor in Latin America and Africa (Neupert et al., 2006; World Bank, 2005).

Why Born Globals Internationalize Early

Exhibit 1.1 highlights key internationalization triggers, factors internal to the firm that drive it into international markets from or near its founding. Why and how do born globals internationalize early, with some going international within the first year of their operations? We describe several explanatory factors below.

Export pull. In most countries, there exists substantial demand for a broad mix of products and services. In the absence of competent local suppliers, export pull describes how local buyers satisfy their product needs by sourcing from abroad. In response to this demand, many born globals market products that occupy narrow, cross-national market niches. The pull effect may be initiated by local intermediaries who perceive a specific product-market opportunity, or it may be initiated by end users themselves who become aware of a given foreign supplier.

Export push. Many born globals are managed by internationally oriented entrepreneurs who possess a powerful drive to sell their products abroad. As demonstrated by early commitment of financial, human, and other resources to generating foreign sales, such managers may view much of the world as their marketplace. They apply a push strategy of actively promoting their offerings to foreign intermediaries, who in turn promote the products to final buyers (e.g., Oviatt & McDougall, 1995). Alternatively, many born globals undertake extensive advertising and develop their own sales organizations to promote products directly to foreign buyers. Modern business infrastructure and advanced technologies in communications and transportation facilitate the ability of any firm to target markets outside the home country. For example, AntiTox Corporation, a manufacturer of products that kill toxins in stored grains and other crops, found numerous markets in Latin America. Within the first five years of operations, the firm's founders perceived a strong need in the markets that was not adequately addressed by competitors' products.

Worldwide monopoly position. Some companies are lucky enough to have developed a monopoly or near-monopoly position in a given product, and this advantage, even in the face of small size, translates into competitive advantages in international business. Monopoly power can derive from tacitly owned knowledge, proprietary products or processes, or other assets that are relatively inseparable from the controlling firm. Moreover, some degree of monopoly power accrues, in the short-term at least, to marketers whose products are substantially differentiated from and/or superior to those of competitors. Finally, companies can obtain a degree of monopoly power to the extent they can convince buyers, through marketing and other means, that theirs is the only product of its kind (Porter, 1980).

Product-market conditions necessitating international involvement. Young firms may produce products, components, or parts so specialized that domestic demand proves insufficient. The small size of the domestic market forces such companies to begin selling in foreign countries. For example, this is a common driver of early internationalization among firms founded in small countries in Europe. In other cases, some businesses set up operations abroad in order to obtain resources that are in short supply or of inappropriate quality at home (e.g., Cavusgil, Knight, & Riesenberger, 2008). Management at many born globals are driven to amortize quickly the development costs associated with new and improved products. This is accomplished by selling these goods into as many markets as possible, an approach that necessitates internationalization. In Japan, capital markets for young companies are not as well developed as they are in other countries, and consequently, some born globals establish a presence in the United States to access funding from such sources. Other companies move offshore to access cheap factors of production such as labor.

Superior product offerings. Many born globals emerge initially as product-process based firms that subsequently emerge as international marketers, based on the strength of a superior product that gains acceptance worldwide. Many born globals internationalize on the strength of an innovative, unique, and/or high quality product. Early internationalization may be associated with a significant product breakthrough or innovation. The products may feature advanced technology, substantial added value, superior quality, or unique characteristics. Many of the products offered by born globals have universal appeal. Some born globals possess an internationally recognized technical eminence in a given product category. These attributes are conducive to expanding into foreign markets shortly after company founding.

Global network relationships. The existence of significant global network relationships is another early internationalization trigger. An industrial network is an organizational structure in which a large number of interconnected actors (firms and individuals) are involved in economic activities (production and marketing) that convert resources (inputs) to finished goods, semi-finished goods, and services for consumption by end-users (retails consumers, intermediaries, and other firms). Scholars highlight the critical role played by network relationships in born global internationalization (e.g., Bell, 1995; Coviello & Munro, 1995; Rasmussen, Madsen, & Evangelista, 2001). Early foreign expansion may be facilitated through network linkages with foreign distributors, trading companies, strategic alliance partners, as well as more traditional buyers and sellers and other entities located abroad. Networks develop through foreign business activities, government intervention, or personal contacts of management and comprise inward (e.g., sourcing) as well as outward (e.g., exporting) interactions. Such relations also provide invaluable knowledge to the born global regarding international business methods and opportunities (e.g., Welch & Luostarinen, 1993). Network relationships allow born globals to obtain advantages abroad that are relatively unattainable in the absence of such linkages.

Global niche markets. Narrow market segments that occur in numerous countries simultaneously are also a factor driving the internationalization of born global firms. The globalization of markets has helped stimulate demand in many industries for customized products and services (Dalgic & Leeuw, 1994; Oviatt & McDougall, 1995). Technology facilitates greater specialization and the emergence of small firms that supply products that occupy narrow, cross-national niches. Indeed, with heightened competition in many industries and advances in production technologies, small entrepreneurs are able to leverage specialized knowledge bases to define and serve market segments small enough to go unnoticed by larger rivals. Such knowledge can be applied to generating "niche thinking" in the identification of global niche markets that the small player can own.

CHAPTER 2

Facilitating Factors in the Emergence of Born Global Firms

Born global firms owe their rise to specific facilitating factors in the external environment of the firm. The born global phenomenon is an artifact of the new global marketplace. These young and entrepreneurial firms are responding to worldwide opportunities. Important factors that are facilitating the rise of born globals include globalization, which is driving the emergence of homogenous worldwide demand. In addition, modern information technology and favorable cost economies of communication and transportation have all played important roles. Also instrumental to the rise of born globals are advances in manufacturing technology that allow efficient and economical production of goods on a modest scale. Let's examine these trends in detail.

Globalization

Initially, the most important facilitating factor is *globalization*. The major drivers, dimensions, and consequences of globalization are highlighted in Exhibit 2.1. Globalization encompasses numerous trends, including the worldwide reduction of barriers to trade and investment; the transition to market-based economies in China, India, Russia, and Eastern Europe; growing convergence of buyer lifestyles and preferences worldwide; and the globalization of firms' production and marketing activities. In 1960, cross-border trade was modest—about $100 billion per year. Today, it accounts for a substantial proportion of the world economy, over $10 trillion annually.

Increasingly, these trends allow managers to view the world as an integrated marketplace. Integration and growing interdependence of national economies have both facilitated, and been caused by, growing interdependence of buyers, producers, and suppliers around the world. Such trends stimulate firms to undertake substantial international business activities. For example, Neogen is a born global that makes diagnostic kits to test food safety. Under globalization, word spread about the superiority of Neogen's products, and the firm was able to acquire a worldwide clientele among farmers, veterinarians, and government agencies.

To give a sense of the momentous impact of globalization on the rise of born global firms, it is useful to provide some historical background. The 1930s and early 1940s were characterized by severe restrictions on international trade and investment. In the years following World War II, industrialized countries sought to reduce these barriers and stimulate global commerce. The General Agreement on Tariffs and Trade (GATT), the precursor to the World Trade Organization, was extremely effective in reducing trade barriers around the world. Within this environment, MNEs from Japan, Europe, and the United States emerged to accelerate global commerce. European firms such as Unilever, Philips, Royal Dutch-Shell, British Petroleum, and Bayer organized their businesses by establishing independent subsidiaries in the foreign countries where they did business. Numerous companies developed internationally recognized brand names, including Nestlé, Kraft, John Deere, Sony, Kellogg, Lockheed, Caterpillar, Volkswagen, Coca-Cola, Toshiba, and Levi's. American multinationals such as IBM, Boeing, Texas Instruments, Xerox, and McDonnell Douglas spread out across the globe.

Beginning in the 1960s, growing MNE activity and trade liberalization led to big increases in international trade and investment. Many more firms began to seek cost advantages by locating manufacturing in countries that offered cost advantages. Falling trade barriers and disappearing currency controls stimulated the free flow of capital across national borders, leading to integration of global financial markets (Emmerij, 1992). Meanwhile, buyer preferences and lifestyles began to converge around the world. Raw materials, parts, and components became increasingly standardized—that is, very similar in design and makeup. Consumers in Tokyo, New York, and Paris began to demand similar household goods, clothing, automobiles, and electronics. By emphasizing a common lifestyle, movies and television contributed to the homogenization of consumer preferences. Converging tastes and

Exhibit 2.1. Drivers, Dimensions, and Consequences of Globalization for Born Global Firms

Drivers of Globalization

- Worldwide reduction of barriers to trade and investment
- Transition to market economics and adoption of free trade in China, India, and former Soviet Union countries
- Industrialization, economic development, and modernization of countries worldwide
- Growth and integration of world financial markets
- Advances in technology

↓

Dimensions of Globalization

- Integration and interdependence of national economies
- Rise of regional economic integration blocs such as the North American Free Trade Agreement (NAFTA) area and the European Union
- Growth of global investment and financial flows
- Convergence of buyer lifestyles and preferences worldwide

↓

Consequences of Globalization for Born Global Firms

- Countless new business opportunities around the world
- New risks and intense rivalry from foreign competitors
- More demanding buyers, who source from suppliers worldwide
- Greater emphasis on the need to undertake proactive internationalization
- Internationalization of firms' value chains

global production platforms facilitated sales of standardized products and services to buyers around the world.

By the early 1980s, the pace of growth in trade and investment accelerated. Key trends in this era included the commercialization of personal computers, advances in communication and manufacturing technologies, the collapse of the Soviet Union and ensuing market liberalization in central and Eastern Europe, and the industrialization and modernization efforts of East Asian economies, including China. Growing global competition forced many firms to streamline their operations and cut manufacturing costs. Companies sought economies in procurement and manufacturing by shifting these activities to foreign locations in order to take advantage of national differences in the cost and quality of labor and other inputs. As a result of these trends, the 1980s were characterized by huge increases in foreign direct investment (FDI), especially in capital- and technology-intensive sectors.

The tendency of national governments to reduce trade and investment barriers facilitated the internationalization of many more firms. For example, from the 1980s onward, tariffs on the import of car parts, industrial machinery, electronics components, and countless other products declined nearly to zero in many countries, encouraging freer international exchange of goods and services. Further declines in trade and investment barriers occurred in the early 1990s through the emergence of regional economic integration blocs, such as the European Union (EU) and the North American Free Trade Agreement (NAFTA) area. The EU, in addition to adopting free trade among its members, harmonized monetary policies and adopted common business regulations.

Globalization both compels and facilitates companies to proactively pursue cross-border business activities and international expansion. Going international has become easier than ever before. A few decades ago, international business was largely the domain of large MNEs. But globalization, alongside the emergence of a regulated global marketplace, has created a level playing field that allows firms of any size to participate in international business. Where cross-border business was once mainly undertaken by manufacturing firms, companies in the services sector are also internationalizing, in such industries as banking, transportation, engineering, design, advertising, and retailing.

Our focus is the effect of globalization on born global firms. Globalization is creating abundant international opportunities for new businesses. The forces of globalization both compel and facilitate companies to pursue cross-border business activities and international expansion. Globalization has stimulated countless firms to undertake international investment, production, sourcing, and marketing, as well as to develop cross-border alliances for product development and distribution. Young firms have benefited from increased outsourcing by larger MNEs and the potential to pursue global markets as specialist suppliers to such firms.

Technological Advances

The second critical trend of recent decades has been *technological advances* in information, communications, manufacturing, and transportation technologies. These advances have made it possible for firms, regardless of age, size or resource base, to internationalize and organize operations around the world. Thanks to technological advances, born globals and international SMEs have gained the ability to view the world as a huge, integrated marketplace.

Advances in information and communications technologies have been particularly noteworthy. In recent decades, the cost of computer processing has fallen by as much as 30% per year and continues to fall. Firms integrate information technologies into their value chains to more efficiently manage production and marketing activities. Advances in telephony, satellites, wireless technology and the Internet have made internationalization viable for countless firms.

Until the 1990s, communicating with foreign suppliers, distributors, and customers was costly or time-consuming, typically accomplished via old-style telex machines and the postal service. In 1980, a 3-minute phone call between New York and London typically cost $6. Today, by using Internet-based systems such as Skype, the call is essentially free. Scanners and fax machines send documents worldwide at practically zero cost. Banking transactions are virtually free when handled via the Internet. Intranets, extranets, and e-mail connect millions of people across the world. The dot-com revolution led to massive investment in fiber optic telecommunications. Transmitting voice, data, and images is essentially costless, making Berlin, Boston, and Bangalore instant next-door neighbors.

Communications technologies have substantially shrunk the geographic and cultural distances that separate nations. Firms leverage communications technologies to minimize costs and maximize operational effectiveness in global value chains. Geographically distant subsidiaries and partners are connected via intranets, facilitating the instant sharing of data, information, and experience across company units worldwide. Being constantly linked to suppliers and distributors greatly increases the effectiveness of managing inventory, product specifications, and purchase orders.

Whereas costly travel or branch offices were once necessary for doing business abroad, technology now brings distant transactions inside the home office of even the smallest firm. E-mail and global cellular telephones facilitate mobile computing and communications, which permit firms to compete anywhere without establishing expensive branch offices. Such systems provide important competitive advantages to born global firms, allowing them to efficiently transact business with upstream and downstream channel members throughout the world.

Information and communications technologies also facilitate online integration and coordination of marketing activities. Technology allows managers to perform online searches, accessing unlimited data for researching markets, customers, competitors, and countries' economic conditions. Direct selling to end users has become much easier. The widest range of products and services—from bank loans to flower pots—is marketed online. Small, flexible firms often can accommodate real-time changes in market conditions almost as quickly as they occur. Many companies become "multinational" by launching sophisticated homepages on the Internet. Exhibit 2.2 describes the various ways in which born globals use the Internet and e-business to succeed in international business.

Important advances have also occurred in manufacturing technologies. Technological developments allow smaller firms to compete more effectively with foreign competitors who already have cost advantages. Advances in production technologies based on microprocessor controls enable low-cost, small-scale manufacturing in many industries. Revolutionary developments permit low-scale and low-cost manufacturing. Technology allows companies to efficiently adapt products for international markets or produce goods in smaller lots to target international niche markets. Marketers segment consumers into narrow global niches and efficiently serve the specialized needs of buyers worldwide. Electronic procurement systems save money on transaction processing, reduce cycle times, and leverage supplier relations.

In transportation, technological advances have occurred in jet aircraft, giant ocean-going freighters, and containerized shipping, often through the use of high-tech composites and smaller components that are light-weight and less bulky. Lower freight costs translate into further advan-tages for small firms in international trade. Express delivery firms such as DHL and FedEx have leveraged advances in transportation and com-munications technologies to slash costs in international shipping. Cost-effective carriers, electronic tracking, containerization, and other efficient systems have become commonplace. Advantaged technologies have greatly increased the reliability of transportation scheduling and arrival times. Managers can now estimate transportation costs and pricing with unprecedented accuracy.

The Role of E-Business in the International Success of Born Global Firms

Information technology and the Internet are transforming interna-tional business by allowing born global firms to conduct e-commerce online as well as integrate e-business capabilities for activities such as sourcing and managing customer relations. Electronic business drives the firm's globalization efforts by helping it beat geography and time zones. E-business levels the playing field for born globals, allowing even the youngest and least experienced firms to expand abroad. Born-global firms are among the most intensive users of the Web for global selling, procurement, and customer service.

E-business provides at least three types of benefits to born global firms. First, it increases productivity and reduces costs in international value-chain activities via online integration and coordination of pro-duction, marketing, and distribution.

Second, e-business creates value for customers and uncovers new sales opportunities by increasing customer focus, enhancing market-ing capabilities, and launching entrepreneurial initiatives. A key ben-efit is the ability to implement marketing strategy on an international scale and integrate customer-focused operations worldwide. Virtual interconnectedness facilitates the sharing of new ideas and best practices for serving new and existing international markets.

Third, e-business improves the flow of information and knowledge among the firm's operations at home and abroad. The Internet allows born globals to process information quickly and to interact more effectively with customers, suppliers, and partners. Managers can make instantaneous changes to strategies and tactics in the firm's international activities.

Born globals can accommodate real-time changes in market conditions almost as quickly as they occur. For example, the firm might use e-business solutions to minimize costs and maximize operational effectiveness in its international supply chain. Numerous born globals use the Internet to maintain regular contact with suppliers and distributors. E-business technologies help born globals manage inventory, product specifications, and purchase orders, as well as product life cycles. E-procurement systems helps firms save money on transaction processing, reduce cycle times, and leverage supplier relations.

Customer relationship management is especially critical in foreign markets where buyers often favor local vendors. Internet-based systems provide real-time information, forecast shifting short- and long-term market needs, and increase the effectiveness of after-sales service. E-commerce enhances the means for firms to achieve competitive advantages and performance objectives in a global marketplace.

Implications of Globalization and Technological Advances for Born Global Firms

The twin trends of globalization and technological advances have created many incentives today for smaller companies to internationalize. Globalization and technological advances support born globals to engage in R&D, procurement, production, and marketing activities on a global scale. Globalization and technological advances gave rise to the "death of distance" (The Death of Distance, 1995). The geographic and cultural distances that separate nations are shrinking. In this way, globalization is making the world a manageable global marketplace for all types of firms.

Young companies are responding to challenges and exploiting new advantages. As preferences for many products converge across markets, these firms sell their offerings throughout the world. They also profit from globalization to source raw materials, parts, components, and service inputs from suppliers located around the globe.

Many born globals seek internationalization proactively also as a result of various internal forces (e.g., pursuit of growth, customers, or to minimize dependence on the domestic market through geographic diversification). Given growing competition in many industries, firms proactively internationalize as a strategic move. They display a more aggressive attitude toward identifying foreign market opportunities, seeking partnerships with foreign firms, and building organizational capabilities to enhance competitive advantage.

Modern technologies, living standard improvements, and adoption of modern legal and banking practices are increasing the attractiveness of emerging markets as target markets and facilitating the spread of products and services across the globe. Modernization of world financial markets and banking services facilitate cross-border transactions due to the ease with which funds can be transferred between buyers and sellers via networks of international commercial banks. For example, foreign customers easily transfer funds to firms using sophisticated banking networks. The globalization of finance enables companies to pay suppliers and collect payments from customers worldwide.

The combination of globalization and advancing technologies has given rise to the emergence of a distinctive breed of entrepreneurial firm, capable of succeeding in the highly competitive environment of international trade. Among the firms that have benefited from globalization and advancing technologies is Geo Search, a Japanese company that develops high-technology equipment to help engineers survey ground surfaces for cavities and build safe roads, airports, and underground utility lines (Rahman, 1999). Using this technology Geo Search designed the world's first land mine detector. The firm had an immediate international market because of millions of mines buried in countries like Kuwait, Cambodia, Afghanistan, and Lebanon. Geo Search works with nongovernmental organizations (NGOs) to search for mines worldwide. Removing land mines is risky, particularly plastic mines that cannot be found with metal detectors. Geo Search's electromagnetic radar can distinguish between mines and other objects buried underground.

Since the 1980s, companies that internationalize at or near their founding have been emerging all around the world. Despite the scarce resources that characterize most small firms, born global managers tend to see the world as their marketplace from or near the firm's founding. Management targets products and services to a dozen or more countries within a few years after launching the firm. The widespread emergence of born globals is exciting because it shows that any company, regardless of its size, age, or resource base, can participate actively in international business.

CHAPTER 3

Literature Review on Born Global Firms

One of the distinguishing characteristics of born globals is the early age at which they venture abroad. In contrast to the pattern of companies that never internationalize, or those that operate domestically for many years and then gradually expand abroad, management at born globals typically has a "borderless" view of the world, from or near the founding of the firm. In this chapter, we review key explanations on born global firms from scholarly journals and books. Exhibit 3.1 summarizes the major themes in the extant academic literature and articles in this literature that represent these themes.

In the 1980s, scholars began to notice the tendency of some companies to undertake early internationalization. In what might have been the earliest study to investigate this phenomenon, Hedlund and Kverneland (1985) examined the entry of Swedish firms into Japan. Among such businesses in the early 1980s, they found that entry and growth strategies were shifting toward more direct and rapid entry modes. About half the firms in the study went directly from an import agent to manufacturing in Japan, without establishing a sales subsidiary (Hedlund & Kverneland, 1985). In essence, the firms undertook early and rapid internationalization. Findings revealed that knowledge about the target foreign market—in the form of existing relations with local agents, licensing methods, and relations with joint venture partners—all supported rapid market entry. Early internationalization was also associated with significant international business experience in the company founders (Hedlund & Kverneland, 1985).

Hedlund and Kverneland (1985) argued that their results cast doubt on the traditional view that companies internationalize slowly and gradually (e.g., Johanson & Vahlne, 1976). They suggested that long-held internationalization views should be revised to account for differing environmental conditions (for example, the increasing similarity of industrialized countries), as well as improvements in firms' ability to manage the complexities of international business. Hedlund and Kverneland (1985) recommended that the benefits of rapid learning and entering a market early should be weighed against the lower risks and other possible advantages associated with more cautious entry strategies. Findings suggested that managers should consider moving more quickly and directly to ambitious forms of representation in foreign markets, as opposed to conventional approaches (Hedlund & Kverneland, 1985).

In 1989, Ganitsky investigated "firms established expressly from their inception to serve foreign markets (innate exporters)" in Israel. He contrasted "innate exporters" with companies that first serve domestic markets and later expand into foreign markets ("adoptive exporters"). Findings from Ganitsky's study revealed that the two types of exporters differ in terms of their assessment processes, reasons for export involvement, risk profiles, and managerial attitudes. Innate exporters were found to surmount internationalization challenges via flexible managerial attitudes and practices. Ganitsky (1989) may have developed the first taxonomy of born global firms when he specified four competitive postures in such firms (leaders, challengers, high performers, and nichers). The limited resources and experiences of innate exporters can inhibit their success. Accordingly, the most successful firms were found to be the adoptive exporters, flexible firms that modify their approaches to suit conditions in individual foreign markets (Ganitsky, 1989).

Born global scholar Patricia McDougall first examined early internationalization in the late 1980s. In an early study (1989), she defined

Major Theme	References
Early Research on Born Global Firms	Hedlund and Kverneland (1985); Ganitsky (1989); McDougall (1989); Rennie (1993); Oviatt & McDougall (1994); Knight and Cavusgil (1995); Knight and Cavusgil (1996); Knight (1997)
Early Internationalization	McDougall, Oviatt, and Shrader (2003); Moen and Servais (2002); McDougall, Oviatt, and Shrader (2003); Bell, McNaughton, Young, and Crick (2003); McNaughton (2003); Chetty and Campbell-Hunt (2004); Mathews and Zander (2007); Fernhaber, McDougall, and Oviatt (2007); Zhou (2007); Kudina, Yip, and Barkema (2008)

General Characteristics of Born Global Firms	Knight (2000); Etemad (2004); Rialp, Rialp, and Knight (2005); Luostarinen and Gabrielsson (2006); Servais, Zucchella, and Palamara (2006); Fan and Phan (2007); Acedo and Jones (2007); Freeman and Cavusgil (2007)
Role of Information and Communications Technologies in Born Global Firms	Loane (2006); Servais, Madsen, and Rasmussen (2007); Zhang and Tansuhaj (2007)
Strategies of Born Global Firms	Knight, Madsen, and Servais (2004); Knight and Cavusgil (2005); Freeman, Edwards, and Schroder (2006); Laanti, Gabrielsson, and Gabrielsson (2007); Mudambi and Zahra (2007); Kuivalainen, Sundqvist, and Servais (2007); Aspelund, Madsen, and Moen (2007); Michailova and Wilson (2008)
Born Globals Explained via the Resource-based and Capabilities Views	Yeoh (2000); Yeoh (2004); Rialp and Rialp (2006); Weerawardena, Mort, Liesch, and Knight (2007); Karra, Phillips and Tracey (2008); Di Gregorio, Musteen, and Thomas (2008)
Born Globals Explained via the Network View of International Business	Sharma and Blomstermo (2003); Mort and Weerawardena (2006); Coviello and Cox (2006); Coviello (2006); Zhou, Wu, and Luo (2007)

Exhibit 3.1. Major Themes and Key References from the Academic Literature on Born Global Firms

"international entrepreneurship" as the emergence of companies that, from their founding, engage in international business. In a study of 188 young firms, McDougall (1989) found that the strategy and industry structure profiles of born global type firms varied substantially from those of domestic new ventures. The international start-ups emphasized aggressive foreign market entry. Management was found to view their operating domain as international from the firm's earliest days. They pursued broad strategies by developing and controlling numerous distribution channels, serving numerous customers in diverse market segments, and developing high market or product visibility (McDougall, 1989).

In 1993, Rennie introduced the term "born global" to describe companies that internationalize at or near their founding. We summarized Rennie's (1993) seminal article in chapter 1. In 1994, Oviatt and McDougall provided the first substantive explanation in the academic literature of born global firms (which they term "international new ventures"). They presented an explanatory framework of early internationalizing firms by integrating accepted MNE and international business theories with developments in entrepreneurship research. They noted that many smaller international firms succeed via control over unique resources, especially knowledge (Oviatt & McDougall, 1994). In a related article, McDougall, Shane, and Oviatt (1994) compared five generally accepted perspectives—Monopolistic Advantage Theory (Hymer, 1976), Product Cycle Theory (Vernon, 1966), Stage Theory of Internationalization (e.g., Bilkey & Tesar, 1977; Cavusgil, 1982), Oligopolistic Reaction Theory (Knickerbocker, 1973), and Internalization Theory (Buckley & Casson, 1976)—and concluded that some aspects of born global firms are not well explained by extant international business theories.

We began writing about born global firms in the mid-1990s (e.g., Knight & Cavusgil, 1995, 1996). We examined studies that supported the existence of early internationalizing firms. In France, for example, Roux (1979) reported on 12 companies that started exporting within three years of their founding. In Canada, Garnier (1982) found numerous companies that had begun exporting at or near their inception. We argued that the born global phenomenon challenges traditional views of company internationalization (e.g., Johanson & Vahlne, 1976). We described born globals, the factors and implications associated with their arrival, and the possible limitations posed for conventional internationalization views (Knight & Cavusgil, 1996).

In 1997, Knight wrote a doctoral dissertation on born globals. He described the born global phenomenon, contrasted such companies with traditional international firms, developed and tested a theoretical model that described key orientations and strategies antecedent to international performance in the born globals, developed and refined "global orientation," a construct relevant to born globals, and generally sought to offer a contemporary explanation on the internationalization of the firm (Knight, 1997).

In the course of researching born global firms, numerous scholars have sought to explain the phenomenon of early internationalization. For example, researchers argue that the level of an industry's global integration and the extent of competing firms' internationalization are likely factors that influence the earliness with which new companies venture abroad (e.g., McDougall, Oviatt, & Shrader, 2003). Using SME exporters from Denmark, Norway, and France, Moen and Servais (2002) found that firms that internationalize early often outperform those that wait several years before expanding abroad. Their results indicated that the firm's future international involvement is influenced by its behavior shortly after company founding. Moen and Servais (2002) highlighted the role of developing appropriate resources and competences that support early internationalization and the ability of young firms to succeed in foreign markets.

Bell, McNaughton, Young, and Crick (2003) highlighted that company internationalization has long been viewed as an incremental process, in which firms gravitate toward "psychically close" markets and increase commitment to international markets via gradual, evolutionary steps. However, the authors noted that born globals appear to challenge this conventional thinking. Internationalization may be triggered by changes in organizational human or financial resources, such as changes in ownership or management, or being taken over by another firm with substantial international networks. The authors (Bell et al., 2003) then proposed an integrative model that recognized various internationalization "pathways" in different types of firms. The model highlighted the role of factors (such as sophisticated knowledge) both inside and outside the firm that foster early internationalization. The authors also examined the role of public policy in fostering and supporting born global firms (Bell et al., 2003).

Recalling traditional internationalization models (e.g., Johanson & Vahlne, 1976), McNaughton (2003) noted that firms usually increase the number of foreign markets into which they expand at a gradual pace. In contrast, born globals typically enter numerous foreign markets at around the same time, at or near the firm's founding. The results of a survey of SME exporters suggest that the more the firm possesses proprietary and knowledge-intensive products, is a member of an industry with a strong global orientation, and is founded in a country with a small domestic market, the more likely it is to target numerous foreign markets (McNaughton, 2003).

Chetty and Campbell-Hunt (2004) investigated young firm internationalization in New Zealand. Case studies revealed that the internationalization paths of traditional versus born global firms differed mainly in the strategies they used and in their prior motivations and capabilities. Among born globals, the authors detected a relatively aggressive learning style that actively seeks engagement and experimentation in international markets, tolerates initial failure, and aggressively seeks solutions to problems as they arise. A proactive learning style helps firms deal effectively with the uncertainty and turbulence of rapid and early internationalization. Chetty and Campbell-Hunt (2004) also argued that born global international expansion is consistent in many ways with traditional views of company internationalization.

Mathews and Zander (2007) investigated the entrepreneurial dynamics of accelerated internationalization. They argued that the salient features of rapid and early internationalization are best captured at the intersection of the entrepreneurship and internationalization perspectives. They discussed their framework in terms of the discovery of new opportunities, the deployment of resources in the exploitation of these opportunities, and engagement with competitors (Mathews & Zander, 2007).

Fernhaber, McDougall, and Oviatt (2007) drew on scholarly literature from industrial economics, entrepreneurship, and international business to identify industry structure variables that help explain born global firms. The authors argued that young companies that operate in industries characterized by rapid growth are more likely to internationalize than new ventures operating in an emerging or mature industry. They also suggested that the greater the knowledge-intensity of an industry, the more likely new firms operating in that industry will internationalize. Firms operating in global, or highly internationalized industries, are more likely to venture abroad at or near their founding. Externally available resources are also highly influential. For example, in industries in which venture capital is widely available, new firms will be more likely to internationalize early (Fernhaber et al., 2007).

In addressing early internationalization, Zhou (2007) highlighted the role of organizational knowledge. In early internationalizing firms, foreign market knowledge tends to emanate from the innovative and proactive pursuit of entrepreneurial opportunities. In traditional international firms, the knowledge usually emerges from the incremental accumulation of experience in foreign markets. Using survey data from young firms in China, Zhou (2007) delineated three dimensions of entrepreneurial proclivity, and found that proactiveness in particular is the most influential, followed by innovativeness. The risk-taking dimension was found to be least influential, perhaps because risk-taking proclivity is more related to managers' perception of the cost of internationalization rather than the accumulation of market knowledge. Zhou (2007) suggested that these results imply that entrepreneurial proclivity and its subdimensions should be treated separately when investigating early internationalization.

Kudina, Yip, and Barkema (2008) examined born globals in Britain and found that the primary reason for early internationalization appeared to be the size of the domestic UK market. The finding is striking in that Britain has one of the largest economies in the world. The drawback of a smaller home market appears to push high-tech UK firms to internationalize early. Based on these findings, the authors argued that rationale for the emergence of born globals might differ for firms based in large markets (such as Japan or the United States), medium-sized markets (such as Britain), and small markets (such as Belgium; Kudina et al., 2008). Another important driver for early internationalization was the need to target the multinational customers common to high-technology industries. The authors also highlighted the presence of global networks and alliances, homogenization of buyer needs around the world, and advances in communication technologies as important factors pushing firms to internationalize early (Kudina et al., 2008).

Numerous studies have described other characteristics of born global firms. For example, Knight (2000) investigated the interrelationships of entrepreneurial orientation, marketing strategy, and firm performance among small international firms affected by globalization. Results indicated that entrepreneurial orientation is associated with the development of specific types of marketing strategies that enhance international performance. The study suggested that born globals strongly affected by globalization appear to emphasize acquisition of useful technologies, responding to internationalization and preparing to enter foreign markets (Knight, 2000).

Etemad (2004) reviewed theory and key factors that influence the internationalization and foreign market success of young, entrepreneurial firms. Among the most critical factors include the direct effect of the entrepreneur on company action, particularly managerial experience and international orientation. Other internal factors that drive internationalization include the economics of operations, characteristics of competitors, the economics of R&D and innovation, and the strategic logic of the firm's international operations. External factors that drive the internationalization of born globals include the liberalization of international markets, advances in information and communications technologies, resources of foreign partners, and the attractiveness of current suppliers and buyers. Other factors that influence internationalization include the ease of expanding abroad, prospects for improving economies of scale, the need to respond to the internationalization of formerly domestic customers, and the need to preserve the firm's previous competitive position. Etemad (2004) also examined the nature of the firm's need for financial resources and dynamic learning-oriented processes in company internationalization (Etemad, 2004).

In their comprehensive review on born global firms, Rialp, Rialp, and Knight (2005) suggested the most common factors which trigger early internationalization include (1) new market conditions in world markets (e.g., the emergence of global niche markets); (2) technological developments in the areas of production, transportation, and communication; (3) the increased importance of global networks and alliances; and (4) the capabilities of firms and the entrepreneurs who found them. Rialp, Rialp, and Knight (2005) also identified several characteristics as critical factors in the early internationalization and success of born global firms. These include (1) presence of founders or managers with a substantial degree of previous international experience; (2) a managerial global vision from inception; (3) strong managerial commitment to succeeding abroad; (4) reliance on personal and business networks, especially in foreign markets; (5) superior knowledge of, and commitment to, foreign markets; (6) unique intangible assets within the firm, rooted in specific knowledge and capabilities; (7) the creation and marketing of high-value offerings, often including leading technology products or goods that emphasize superior quality; (8) pursuit of a global niche strategy that emphasizes narrow market segments that span numerous countries; (9) strong market orientation and focus on customers; and (10) flexibility to adapt to rapidly changing conditions and circumstances, particularly in foreign markets (Rialp et al., 2005).

Luostarinen and Gabrielsson (2006) surveyed 89 Finnish companies to examine whether the strategies and processes of born globals differ from other firms regarding internationalization and strategies applied in foreign markets. The authors classified born global internationalization into three preliminary stages (R&D, domestic phase, and foreign market entry) and into four major stages (starting, development, growth, and maturity). They also examined the international marketing strategies of born globals via case studies on 30 firms representing the above stages. The authors found that mature born globals had passed quickly through the conventional internationalization stages (e.g., Cavusgil, 1980; Johanson & Vahlne, 1977) and jumped over some stages. The authors cast their findings in the context of companies originating in small and open economies (Luostarinen & Gabrielsson, 2006).

Luostarinen and Gabrielsson (2006) note that the young founders of born globals are often "forward-going and fearless." They are typically self-starters who hire young and educated people (often individual with little business experience) to manage the firm. Born global founders also often have strong backgrounds in technology or research and some are former employees of downsized businesses. In addition to internal resources, cooperating with external partners to undertake R&D, marketing and production compensate for the dearth of resources in born global firms. Some firms employ consultants or outsource tasks to outside suppliers. Born globals often use the Internet to support their marketing activities. The authors also highlight various public policy ideas regarding born global firms (Luostarinen & Gabrielsson, 2006). Finally, they note that the traditional stages models of company internationalization (e.g., Cavusgil, 1980; Johanson & Vahlne, 1977) continue to hold much explanatory value in research on born globals (Luostarinen & Gabrielsson, 2006).

Servais, Zucchella, and Palamara (2006) focused on international sourcing as an entrepreneurial act and demonstrated that it is often a critical factor in the internationalization processes of small firms, both established and new ventures. The authors investigated how these firms, characterized typically by scarce financial and managerial resources, can successfully manage international value chains. The authors investigate the breadth of international sourcing activities and the nature of the ties established under arms-length sourcing agreements. The study found that small firms—whether they internationalize late or early—are widely involved in global sourcing activity (Servais et al., 2006).

The origin of the firm, including the characteristics of founders and resources prior to founding, can strongly influence management's proclivity for taking risks, proactiveness in foreign markets, and other factors that determine organizational performance during internationalization. Scholars have found that prior international experience is conducive to early internationalization (McDougall et al., 2003). Managers with preexisting international experience bring potentially much knowledge to the born global about the international business environment and how to organize the firm for optimal operations in foreign markets.

Fan and Phan (2007) examined the pattern of born global entry into international markets and suggested that born globals are not necessarily a distinctive breed of firms. However, several factors appear to be very influential in supporting the early internationalization of the firm. These include having a superior technological advantage, the size of the firm's home market, its production capacity, as well as cultural and economic forces in the firm's external environment. The authors demonstrate that the decision to be born global is influenced by the size of the home market and by the firm's inaugural production capacity, as well as the level of competition in target markets (Fan & Phan, 2007).

Acedo and Jones (2007) examined four aspects of managers' cognitive patterns, as differentiated by speed of international market entry. The aspects were risk perception, proactivity, tolerance for ambiguity, and international orientation. Using data from 216 firms, the authors found that risk perception affects firms' proclivity for rapid internationalization (Acedo & Jones, 2007). However, the extent of risk perception, and reaction to perceived risk, is influenced by the nature of managers' proactive posture, international orientation, and tolerance for ambiguity. A highly international orientation appears to foster higher levels of proactivity and lower perceptions of risk in internationalization. The authors conjectured that internationally oriented managers are better informed and more likely to behave proactively and be less concerned about risk regarding internationalization opportunities. Increasing the international orientation of managers may lower perceptions of risk (Acedo & Jones, 2007). This points to a role for hiring individuals with substantial international experience and language abilities or providing training, travel, and other opportunities to gain knowledge appropriate for international operations.

Freeman and Cavusgil (2007) advanced theoretical explanations regarding the behavior of born global firms. In an Australian case-based study, the authors focus on the attitudinal orientations of senior managers. They sought to integrate the network perspective and resource-based view with international entrepreneurship (Freeman & Cavusgil, 2007). Their exploration of the mind-set of company personnel identified four states of commitment to accelerated internationalization by top management. The most advanced of these is the "strategist" state, in which managers adopt a collaborative behavioral stance aimed at developing and preserving key relationships that facilitate internationalization. The strategist seeks to continually build network links into lead markets and regions for locating and serving key foreign customers and suppliers globally. The strategist also emphasizes the development of trust, reciprocity, and adaptability in venturing abroad, viewing internationalization as an innovative process (Freeman & Cavusgil, 2007).

A few studies have investigated the role of information and communications technologies in the international performance of born global firms. Loane (2006) examined the role of the Internet in the internationalization of small entrepreneurial firms from various countries. Born globals use the Internet for communication, for marketing communications, and, to a lesser degree, for managing customer relationships as well as sales transactions and fulfillment activities. Most of the investigated firms also used the Internet to support off-line sales, and about one-quarter used the Internet to support distribution channels and intermediaries (Loane, 2006). A significant number of firms used the Internet to support relations with partners, suppliers, clients, agents and distributors, R&D partners, and software coding developers, both nationally and internationally. The born globals also used the Internet as a tool for acquiring knowledge, such as market and competitive intelligence, which then become part of the collective wisdom of the firm (Loane, 2006).

Servais, Madsen, and Rasmussen (2007) investigated the role of electronic business in the internationalization of SMEs. They found the Internet makes borders between countries less relevant and facilitates direct interaction between all types of business entities around the world. The authors highlighted Internet usage by born globals compared to other types of firms. They concluded that born globals use the Internet to convey their market presence abroad, support relationships with foreign partners, offer services related to their products, facilitate product development, and maintain relations with foreign customers (Servais et al., 2007).

Zhang and Tansuhaj (2007) conducted in-depth interviews with managers, coupled with public database and Web site searches, to develop a collection of research propositions regarding born global firms. They investigated the relationship between organizational culture, information technology capability, and international performance in these firms. The paper employed a case research approach to argue that effective utilization of information technology supports and shapes the strategies of born global firms. Information technology capability is effective in enhancing company performance. Moreover, findings suggest that market orientation, international entrepreneurial orientation, and organizational learning are key organizational cultures that foster the development of information technology capability in these firms (Zhang & Tansuhaj, 2007). Using the resource-based view of the firm (e.g., Barney, 1991; Collis, 1991; Wernerfelt, 1984), the authors argued that information technology capability is an important resource and a source of competitive advantage of born globals (Zhang & Tansuhaj, 2007). If leveraged well, the capability leads to superior international performance. However, it is critical for managers to skillfully mobilize and deploy information technology in combination with their other resources and capabilities. Organizational culture is also critical, and the firm should focus on developing capabilities in areas such as market orientation, organizational learning capacity, and international entrepreneurial orientation (Zhang & Tansuhaj, 2007).

Numerous studies have highlighted the specific strategies applied by born global firms. Knight, Madsen, and Servais (2004) investigated marketing-related strategies. Using case and survey-based data from Denmark and the United States, the authors developed a structural model that suggested born globals' international performance is enhanced by foreign customer focus and marketing competence. Marketing competence implies skillful handling of product adaptation and the marketing planning process, control of marketing activities, prowess in differentiating the product, as well as being highly effective in pricing, advertising, and distribution (Knight et al., 2004). The firms focused on their customers and this focus drove key marketing strategies and helped to maximize customer value. Born globals are characterized by limited resources, and focus strategy helps them employ their resources with maximal efficiency. Product quality and differentiation strategy also played important roles. Management at the investigated firms was also strongly internationally oriented (Knight et al., 2004).

In a 2005 empirical study of several hundred companies, we developed a taxonomy and found four broad clusters of born global firms, particularly in terms of the strategies they follow (Knight & Cavusgil, 2005). Born globals in the first cluster had a strong entrepreneurial and strategic focus, as well as superior international performance. These firms especially excelled in differentiation and focus strategies (Porter, 1980). Cluster two firms were also strong in focus and differentiation and in technological leadership. Cluster three's main strategy was cost leadership. However, firms that compete on low costs alone are subject to price competition, which puts pressure on profit margins. Such firms are typically less profitable and are vulnerable to competitor moves that pull customers away (e.g., Porter, 1980). Given the competitive position of most born globals—smaller on average and having few scale advantages—emphasis on cost leadership strategy is ill-advised. Based on study findings, it appears that most born globals perform better by avoiding approaches in which cost leadership is the sole source of competitive advantage (Knight & Cavusgil, 2005). Indeed, in the study, both clusters three and four emphasized cost leadership and were generally the poorest performers. By contrast, cluster two firms (which emphasize focus and differentiation strategies) and cluster one firms (which emphasized other approaches as their main strategies) enjoyed superior international performance. Cluster four firms did not typify any particular strategic pattern. Their primary characteristic was an absence of a distinctive strategic competence, a condition reminiscent of Porter's (1980) "stuck in the middle" category, and therefore unlikely to achieve substantial profits. Overall study findings suggested that born globals need a well-defined strategic orientation. In terms of generic strategies, focus or differentiation appear to be particularly appropriate (Knight & Aulakh, 1998; Knight & Cavusgil, 2005).

Freeman, Edwards, and Schroder (2006) identified constraints that confront born global firms, particularly lack of resources, insufficient economies of scale, and aversion to risk-taking. The authors explored how born globals overcome these constraints by employing technology to achieve competitive advantages and by leveraging networking competencies to develop alliances and collaborative partnerships. The article described how small firms achieve rapid growth internationally via alliances with distributors, suppliers and other partners (Freeman et al., 2006). The authors emphasized that born globals can overcome constraints to international business when there is a strong commitment by senior management to internationalization; personal networks that provide the basis for establishing useful partnerships and alliances; unique technology that provides competitive advantages; a commitment to growth through partnerships with suppliers and distributors; a willingness to adapt relationships to meet the changing needs of partners; and using the appropriate entry strategy for each foreign market (Freeman et al., 2006).

Laanti, Gabrielsson, and Gabrielsson (2007) discussed the globalization process of business-to-business born globals in the wireless technology industry, which can be viewed as a surrogate for other high-tech industries. In this context, the authors analyzed the roles of the founders and managers, the networks, financial resources, and the innovations behind the companies under consideration. They explored the product, market, and operational strategies of born global firms. Findings revealed that born globals deviate from the traditional internationalization process in many areas. They apply rapid internationalization even to distant markets or very different markets. They employ advanced product strategies at an early stage of internationalization (Laanti et al., 2007). The authors also emphasized the role of the resources and capabilities of born globals in the development of product categories, operation strategies, and global market presence. As born globals are typically small and disadvantaged, they often obtain needed resources from their external domestic and international networks or via the earlier experience and collective knowledge of the firm's founding managers (Laanti et al., 2007).

Mudambi and Zahra (2007) examined the survival of born globals in the context of advanced foreign market entry modes, such as FDI. Findings suggested that the early or rapid internationalization of born globals does not necessarily produce a higher rate of company failure than the sequential internationalization followed by traditional international firms. Born globals that enter markets characterized by high rates of growth are typically more successful than firms that target slower growing markets. Born globals with higher levels of technological competence are more likely to survive and thrive in foreign markets. Finally, larger firms are more likely to perform better than smaller companies (Mudambi & Zahra, 2007). Based on study findings, the authors argued that firms should judiciously devise appropriate strategies and entry approaches before entering foreign markets early after their founding. Knowledge about the social and market conditions of target markets substantially improves the odds of successfully implementing chosen market entry modes. Managers should effectively exploit their firms' intangible resources, such as technological competences, as they consider internationalizing their operations (Mudambi & Zahra, 2007).

Kuivalainen, Sundqvist, and Servais (2007) reviewed the literature on born globals and explored the relationship between entrepreneurial orientation and born global strategy. Results of an empirical study suggested that the "most born global" of born global firms enjoyed superior export performance. Depending on the degree of the firm's born-globalness, various dimensions of entrepreneurial orientation were particularly important to company success. Results highlighted the critical role of entrepreneurial behavior in the development of international strategy (Kuivalainen et al., 2007).

Aspelund, Madsen, and Moen (2007) examined top academic journals in entrepreneurship, marketing, and management to comprehensively review the literature on born global firms during the years 1992 to 2004. They reviewed findings related to the founding of the firm, organizational characteristics, environmental conditions, and the influence of these factors on market strategy and company performance. The study concluded that recent empirical findings on born globals offer insights beyond traditional internationalization models. More theory-driven research is needed. For example, research on born globals could benefit by applying general organizational theories in an attempt to understand international expansion and market strategies of new firms. The review of articles across numerous journals revealed the following characteristics of born global internationalization and international strategies: speed, heterogeneity with much variation between firms, emphasis on niche focus strategy, strong role for the firm's network and top management experience, a focus on lead markets and growth markets, and entry strategies characterized by low commitment, often with an emphasis on partnering with intermediaries and other facilitators in target markets (Aspelund et al., 2007). The review revealed there is much heterogeneity regarding the international marketing strategies of born globals. Some born globals market niche products while others emphasize commodities. Some firms choose markets based on personal networks while others use different criteria. Some born globals concentrate on a few markets, while others spread out across numerous markets. The authors suggest that the reasons for this heterogeneity in strategies can be found in the founding process of the firm, organizational factors, and environmental conditions (Aspelund et al., 2007).

Michailova and Wilson (2008) highlighted the critical role of experiential learning in small firm internationalization. They investigated the conditions under which experiential learning is most important for internationalization. The authors framed their research within the socialization tactics literature to theorize how the context, content, and social aspects of foreign ventures offer distinctive opportunities for acquiring experiential knowledge to support small firm internationalization. Socialization tactics appear to moderate the relationship between individual international experiential knowledge and small firm internationalization. Opportunities for international experiential learning can be optimized when the socialization context is individual and formal (rather than collective and nonformal), the socialization content is sequential and fixed (rather than random and variable), and when socialization involves serial and investiture (rather than disjunctive and divestiture) social aspects (Michailova & Wilson, 2008).

Recent literature has leveraged the resource-based view (e.g., Barney, 1991; Collis, 1991; Wernerfelt, 1984) and dynamic capabilities view (e.g., Dosi, 1988; Nelson & Winter, 1982; Teece, Pisano, & Shuen, 1997) to explain born global firms. For example, information and knowledge are critical resources in the internationalization of young firms. In her investigation of born global exporters, Yeoh (2000) examined firms' information search efforts. She found that organizational characteristics and strategic orientation, as well as environmental and information source characteristics, are particularly salient for predicting how young firms seek out information as they internationalize. In a follow-up study, Yeoh (2004) examined three kinds of learning that result from internationalization: technological, market, and social. Findings revealed that external networks with suppliers and customers are a major contributor to a firm's international performance. Findings on the influence of market learning on firm performance also support the assumptions underlying the resource-based view of the firm.

Rialp and Rialp (2006) analyzed the effect of various company resources, particularly intangible ones, on the internationalization of born global firms. The authors investigated the role of intangible resources on whether firms internationalize early and whether business results achieved from this activity are superior to those of other, non–born global firms. They based their findings on a representative sample of exporting manufacturers in Spain. Results confirmed that both human and organizational capital resources have a significant impact on the success of born global firms (Rialp & Rialp, 2006).

Dynamic capabilities are the routines through which the firm learns from sources based in the market, the firm's network of relationships, and the learning that is harnessed internal to the firm itself (e.g., Dosi, 1988; Nelson & Winter, 1982; Teece et al., 1997). Weerawardena and colleagues (2007) drew on the dynamic capabilities view to present a conceptual model of born global internationalization. Managerial capabilities sufficient for successful internationalization are often defined by preexisting knowledge and background of the founders. Founder characteristics also help address the issue of why some young firms opt to internationalize from inception, while many others focus on their domestic markets. A set of dynamic capabilities that are built and nurtured by internationally oriented entrepreneurial founders allow these firms to develop leading-edge products that pave the way for their early internationalization (Weerawardena, Mort, Liesch, & Knight, 2007).

Weerawardena et al. (2007) argued that the most critical capabilities in born global internationalization and international performance include a market-focused learning capability, internally focused learning capability, networking capability, and marketing capability. These capabilities in combination with superior qualifications of company founders (such as possession of an international entrepreneurial orientation, prior international experience, and a general learning orientation) lead born globals to develop knowledge intensive products that facilitate early internationalization. The authors suggested that accelerated internationalization is most effective when the firm learns from multiple sources. This learning gives rise to knowledge that management used to advance company performance. Small firms that aspire to early internationalization should develop a strategic set of dynamic capabilities (Weerawardena et al., 2007).

Using a case study approach, Karra, Phillips, and Tracey (2008) proposed three entrepreneurial capabilities that appear particularly important in the success of born global firms: international opportunity identification, institutional bridging, and a capacity and preference for cross-cultural collaboration. "Institutional distance" refers to the differences in business environments that firms encounter as they move from a home to a host country. Institutional bridging refers to the capacity to overcome this distance, for example, by translating business concepts and opportunities between national contexts, and articulating and making them relevant to people in different countries. The authors examined how emergent international entrepreneurs can develop the three entrepreneurial capabilities to improve their chances for international success (Karra et al., 2008).

Just as they leverage internal resources to expand into foreign markets, many born globals internationalize in order to gain access to value-creating resources in various countries. For substantially internationalized firms, important advantages arise when the resources are unevenly distributed across nations, which international firms can then selectively access and combine with internal resources in order to create competitive advantages. Di Gregorio, Musteen, and Thomas (2008) presented a framework for born global firms as the cross-border nexus of individuals and opportunities. Many born globals emerge due to the appearance of opportunities that reflect cross-national combinations of resources and markets. The authors emphasized that active entrepreneurs should extend their search for opportunities in foreign markets beyond the search for potential customers to also actively scan for tangible and intangible resources and opportunities, and combine them in novel, innovative ways.

Several scholars have applied the network view of international business to explain born global firms. For example, Sharma and Blomstermo (2003) proposed that models that emphasize knowledge and networks are particularly appropriate for theory development on the internationalization of born globals. The authors showed that born globals tend to acquire international market knowledge before their first foreign market entry. Management's choice of foreign market entry mode is typically based on its existing knowledge and knowledge supplied by network ties (Sharma & Blomstermo, 2003).

Mort and Weerawardena (2006) examined the role of networks in the development of born global firms in Australia. Study findings suggested that dynamic networking capabilities enable born globals to minimize the risks associated with international market entry decisions. The most successful networking activity is complemented by entrepreneurial opportunity-seeking behaviors (Mort & Weerawardena, 2006).

Coviello and Cox (2006) built on network theory and the resource-based view (e.g., Barney, 1991; Collis, 1991; Wernerfelt, 1984) to explore how networks facilitate resource development in born globals. Using case study data, the authors advanced propositions on the dynamics of organizational, human, physical, financial, and social capital, and the nature of these resource flows as they pertain to born global networks. The authors noted that the types of resources generated via the firm's network evolve as the born global transitions through various internationalization stages (Coviello & Cox, 2006). In the initial stages, born globals leverage their networks to generate organizational skills and competencies, including technological capabilities. After internationalization is well underway, managerial focus shifts to developing human resources to support further growth. Subsequently, the firm shifts its emphasis to building its client and distribution base. For born globals, networks are critical to generating social capital and provide for the acquisition, mobilization, and development of needed resources (Coviello & Cox, 2006).

Coviello (2006) employed network theory and the entrepreneurship literature to present findings on the networks that support the internationalization and success of born global firms. Results of her study confirmed the important role of networks in opening doors for born globals to provide market access, financing, distribution channels, and contacts for both internal and external development. Coviello (2006) noted that resources acquired within the firm's network not only aid the born global as it evolves through internationalization but also before internationalization, from the earliest stage of company development. The study found that the nature of resources obtained from the network can vary from firm to firm, and across the stages of internationalization (Coviello, 2006).

Zhou, Wu, and Luo (2007) offered a social network explanation regarding the relationship between internationalization and performance in born global firms. The authors argued that social networks based in the home market play a mediating role in the relationship between inward and outward internationalization and enterprise performance. Networks of social relationships can serve as the basis from which formal networks of business linkages are developed in new markets, and through which relationships that aid in internationalization are formed. Social networks aid in identifying new opportunities and developing specific competitive advantages via the accumulation of international knowledge. Building and maintaining network relationships is generally critical to the internationalization process, as both outcomes and inputs to the process. Using survey data from SMEs in China, the authors investigated *guanxi*, essentially "connections," and found that business managers should consider social networks as an efficient means of facilitating early and profitable internationalization (Zhou et al., 2007).

CHAPTER 4

Theoretical Explanations and Frameworks on Born Global Firms

Let us now consider specific theories and frameworks that have been applied to explaining born global firms. The founders of born globals are individuals who pursue international opportunities from or near the founding of the firm. They undertake international business from the time of venture formation, developing international competencies and avoiding path-dependence on domestic competencies that the firm may not be able to shift out of due to inertial forces. Scholars have argued that the formation process of born globals is not well explained by existing international business theories (e.g., Knight & Cavusgil, 1995; McDougall et al., 1994). This is partly because traditional perspectives have tended to assume that firms become international long after they have been formed (e.g., Johanson & Vahlne, 1977).

For example, Coviello and McAuley (1999) reviewed empirical research on small firm internationalization, in the context of foreign direct investment theory, the "stages" models of internationalization (e.g., Cavusgil, 1980; Johanson & Vahlne, 1977), and the network perspective. The authors found that when examined independently, these perspectives do not adequately explain the complex internationalization processes that characterize born global firms. The authors concluded that small firm internationalization is better understood by integrating major theoretical frameworks. The three schools of internationalization research should be viewed in a holistic, integrated manner (Coviello & McAuley, 1999).

In the spirit of Coviello and McAuley's work (1999), we focus on specific perspectives that aid in explicating born global firms. As in other scholarly and practical endeavors, certain theories and frameworks hold much value in helping to explain the phenomenon of born global firms. Exhibit 4.1 summarizes major useful theoretical perspectives, orientations, and strategies regarding these companies. Initially, it is useful to examine the role of resources and capabilities in born global internationalization and performance in foreign markets. For example, Oviatt and McDougall (1995) noted that born globals appear to be characterized by management with international vision from or near inception of the firm, superior access to international business networks, and possession of preemptive technologies appropriate for pursuing foreign opportunities.

Preemptive technologies and distinctive intangible assets appear to be particularly important company resources that born globals assemble to support their international activities. In this way, the resource-based view (Barney, 1991; Collis, 1991; Wernerfelt, 1984) has served as one of the most useful perspectives in helping to explain born global firms. This view implies that differential endowment of organizational resources is an important determinant of company strategy and performance (Collis, 1991; Wernerfelt, 1984). Resources are (tangible and intangible) assets that are tied semipermanently to the firm (Wernerfelt, 1984). The resource-based view suggests that specific organizational resources that are valuable, unique, and hard-to-imitate help to separate winners from losers in global competition (Peng & York, 2001).

In addition to financial assets, plant, property, and equipment, resources comprise human, organizational, informational, and relational elements such as the skills and knowledge embedded in company employees. Resources that lead to profitability include assets such as brand names, in-house knowledge, employment of skilled personnel, trade contacts, and efficient procedures (Hunt, 2000; Wernerfelt, 1984). Company culture, capabilities, routines, and processes can be regarded as organizational resources (e.g., Hunt, 2000). When leveraged skillfully, such resources engender organizational efficiency and effectiveness. They result in the development of one or more core competences—vectors of assets along which the firm is uniquely advantaged—that provide substantial competitive advantages and superior sustainable performance. When examined within the resource-based view, born globals are seen to survive and thrive in competitive foreign markets by applying a unique gestalt of managerial and intangible resources, and by aligning key strategic assets with the demands of local markets.

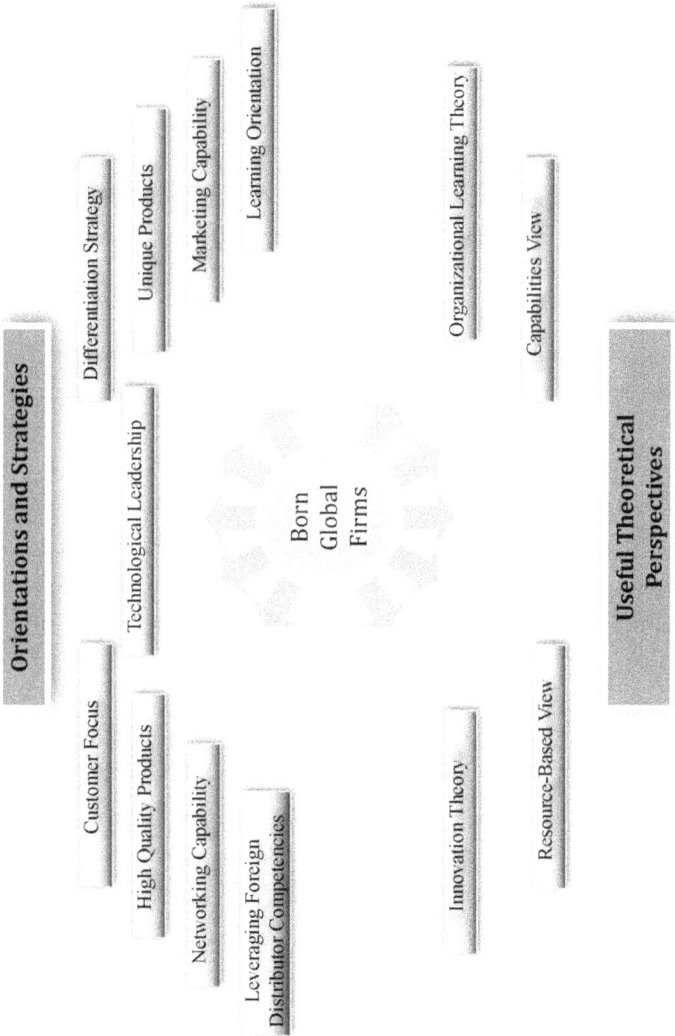

Exhibit 4.1. Useful Theoretical Perspectives, Orientations, and Strategies regarding Born Global Firms

Orientations and Strategies

- Differentiation Strategy
- Unique Products
- Marketing Capability
- Learning Orientation
- Technological Leadership
- Customer Focus
- High Quality Products
- Networking Capability
- Leveraging Foreign Distributor Competencies

Useful Theoretical Perspectives

- Organizational Learning Theory
- Capabilities View
- Innovation Theory
- Resource-Based View

Born Global Firms

The resource-based view rests on two key assumptions: (1) firms in a given industry are heterogeneous with regard to the resources they control, and (2) because resources are not perfectly mobile across firms, heterogeneity tends to be long-lasting (Barney, 1991; Collis, 1991; Hunt, 2000; Mahoney, 1995). Today, many young companies manifest specific resources comprising dispositions and competencies that are instrumental to the conception and implementation of international business. While most such businesses lack the substantial financial and human resources of large MNEs, they hold a collection of other, possibly more fundamental, resources that facilitate their international success. For example, many born globals possess a corporate culture well suited to international business success, a propensity to leverage the latest information and communications technologies, and the flexibility and entrepreneurial drive that are characteristic of innovative young firms.

In order to ensure competitive advantages, it is necessary that company resources be relatively scarce or distinctive (Barney, 1991; Collis, 1991; Hunt, 2000; Mahoney, 1995). Scarcity and distinctiveness can be achieved in several ways. For example, the firm may be relatively unique regarding the nature and extent of specialized knowledge held by individual managers or embedded within the firm. Causal ambiguity and social complexity give rise to the development of specific knowledge and capabilities that are imperfectly imitable by would-be rival firms (Barney, 1991). Competitors might well be able to imitate the visible, tangible resources owned by the firm (e.g., plant, equipment, raw materials) but nearly impossible to imitate idiosyncratic knowledge-intensive orientations, routines, and processes that give rise to particular product offerings or marketing modes. Competitive imitation of such resources is only possible via the same time-consuming process of irreversible investment or knowledge acquisition that the firm itself underwent (Collis, 1991). Managers at rival firms usually lack the knowledge of the particular circumstances, social structure, and causal relationships of the firm within which actions need to be interpreted (Mahoney, 1995). In cases where organizational resources are no better than those of rival firms, core competencies can arise through the superior usage of these resources (Hunt, 2000). The resource-based view suggests that precisely because it is difficult to obtain, a surplus of tacit knowledge can provide the firm with competitive advantages in foreign markets (Liesch & Knight, 1999).

Being young, born globals tend to lack substantial financial and human resources, as well as extensive holdings of property, plants, equipment, and other physical assets. It is these *tangible* resources that older firms typically have relied upon to propel them to international business success. Born globals experience other disadvantages. The youth, inexperience, and newness of these firms to international business can limit management's ability to acquire needed resources that support internationalization. Potential stakeholders are often reluctant to invest in young, unproven firms. In addition, limited tangible resources means that many small firms are often unable to surmount the challenges of internationalization and operating in foreign markets. Born globals must typically struggle to overcome barriers to entry, build links to foreign intermediaries, undertake substantial marketing programs, and gain the acceptance of potential customers. Any of these liabilities can increase the risk of failure for born global firms. A combination of these liabilities tends to magnify the risks.

However, born global firms often leverage a collection of *intangible* resources and capabilities, such as organizational culture and competences, knowledge held by individual employees, and relationships with key channel members, that facilitate their international success. For example, Knight and Cavusgil (2004) found that born globals succeed by acquiring and applying a specific constellation of orientations and strategies. These are intangible resources and capabilities that represent know-how, skills, and experiences held by the managers who work at these firms. Frequently, born globals appear to hold superior tacit knowledge about global opportunities, and the capabilities to leverage such knowledge in ways not matched by competitors.

International business scholars have long emphasized foreign direct investment and the tendency of firms to acquire foreign assets in order to achieve superior international performance. However, born global firms usually succeed without owning substantial resources. Many are "virtual firms" that leverage networks and other relationships to access needed resources (e.g., Coviello & Munro, 1995). The entrepreneurial actions of born globals lie at the core of their ability to create value in ways that distinguish them from competitors endowed with substantial financial and tangible resources. The born global phenomenon reveals how young companies internationalize via "entrepreneurial action" rather than the resources they own or control (e.g., Knight & Cavusgil, 2004). The key to born global success might well be "resourcefulness," as opposed to the sheer volume or quality of the resources under the firm's control. In this way, the born global phenomenon challenges the traditional FDI-oriented view of international business.

Closely related to the resource-based view is the *capabilities view* of the firm (e.g., Eisenhardt & Martin, 2000; Nelson & Winter, 1982). The dynamic capabilities view emphasizes the role of capabilities (as opposed to resources) in explaining the ability of firms to achieve particular organizational goals and objectives. Dynamic capabilities represent the firm's ability to integrate, reconfigure, gain, and release organizational resources. Dynamic capabilities operate to direct organizational resources, operational routines, and competencies toward achieving superior performance in the markets where the firm chooses to operate (e.g., Eisenhardt & Martin, 2000; Nelson & Winter, 1982). The development of superior dynamic capabilities hinges on knowledge-based processes inside the firm, which are instrumental to knowledge creation, knowledge integration, and knowledge configuration (Helfat & Raubitschek, 2000; Zollo & Winter, 2002). Entrepreneurial managers in born global firms function to reform or revolutionize patterns of production by exploiting inventions, innovations, or technologies in ways that open new outlets for the firm's offerings. Possession of appropriate capabilities helps engender the development or improvement of methods for doing business (Dosi, 1988; Nelson & Winter, 1982).

The dynamic capabilities view suggests that the ability to internationalize despite limited company resources is a function of the internal capabilities of the firm (McDougall et al., 1994; Zahra, Ireland, & Hitt, 2000). Dynamic capabilities help firms achieve new resource configurations as markets emerge and evolve (Eisenhardt & Martin, 2000). In addition to introducing new goods, services, and production methods, possession of specific organizational capabilities supports the opening of new markets and reinventing the firm's operations to serve those markets optimally (e.g., Nelson & Winter, 1982). Internationalization, or new entry into markets overseas, is an innovative act (Simmonds & Smith, 1968). Thus, innovatory capacity helps management to devise new strategies and tactics that support performance as the firm expands abroad (e.g., Weerawardena et al., 2007).

Dynamic capabilities do not simply emerge on their own but are developed consciously and systematically by the willful choices and actions of the firm's strategic leaders (Lado, Boyd, & Wright, 1992; Teece et al., 1997). The dynamic capabilities view emphasizes the role of entrepreneurial managerial activities within the firm directed at the development of competitive strategies (e.g., Weerawardena et al., 2007). Dynamic capabilities help management to appropriately adapt, integrate, and reconfigure organizational skills, resources, and functional competences. The term "dynamic" refers to the ability of managers to renew the firm's competences so as to achieve congruence within evolving business environments (Teece et al., 1997). In this sense, dynamic capabilities might be particularly important to born globals because these firms deal largely in the complex, dynamic realm of foreign markets characterized by a range of environments.

Weerawardena et al. (2007) highlight the roles played by market-focused learning capability, internally focused learning capability, and networking capability in the internationalization and international performance of born global firms. Their view is associated with another useful perspective—*organizational learning theory*. Organizational learning concerns the processes involved in assimilating new knowledge into the firm's knowledge base (e.g., Liesch & Knight, 1999). Pursuing international opportunities involves learning about a range of conditions and phenomena often not present in the domestic market. Competitive advantages arise from the knowledge obtained from the firm's exposure to the variety of conditions that exist abroad. For example, significant technological learning can occur through internationalization (Zahra et al., 2000). The resulting advantage is likely to be particularly relevant in knowledge-intensive sectors. Thus, international expansion can promote organizational learning and facilitate the development of skills and competencies that give rise to competitive advantages (Autio et al., 2000; Cohen & Levinthal, 1990).

Given the complexities of foreign markets, internationalizing firms typically must revise or unlearn organizational practices rooted in domestic operations in order to implant new, internationally oriented practices. Unlearning established practices becomes more difficult as firms get older because new knowledge that leads to new practices tends to conflict with existing mindsets and operations (Autio et al., 2000; Barkema & Vermeulen, 1998).

Organizational learning theory suggests that the development of new organizational knowledge occurs best under conditions in which there are little or no existing organizational routines to unlearn (Autio et al., 2000; Cohen & Levinthal, 1990; Nonaka, 1995). Accordingly, less-established firms, such as born globals, may be more adept at acquiring requisite knowledge about international business and more efficient and effective at developing new international activities.

In many born global firms, organizational culture is attuned to operating in markets that are both geographically and psychically distant. Organizational learning theory suggests that the younger a firm is at the time of its international expansion, the better equipped it may be to acquire requisite knowledge about international business. Younger, more agile firms are efficient and effective as they grow into international activities. International expansion promotes organizational learning, which facilitates the development of skills and competencies that help the firm achieve a competitive advantage. Early internationalization confers advantages in terms of knowledge acquisition about international markets and how to succeed in them. Early internationalization can provide numerous learning opportunities that benefit the firm's performance because of the range of environments and competitive situations to which the firm is exposed as it ventures abroad (Autio et al., 2000; Cohen & Levinthal, 1990). Moreover, contact and the development of relationships with various foreign intermediaries also promotes learning. The diversity of international environments offers exposure to new and diverse ideas from multiple market and cultural perspectives and helps the born global progress rapidly up the international learning curve.

In a related sense, a key advantage of born global firms is that they typically lack a long-standing *administrative heritage* characteristic of long-established businesses. In older companies, long-established structures and processes tend to constrain strategic choice. Administrative heritage constrains managerial thinking about possible strategic and tactical choices (e.g., Collis, 1991; Liesch & Knight, 1999). The administrative heritage view suggests how, over time, managers develop their own preferred ways of doing business. Internationalization exposes the firm to a wide variety of complex challenges in diverse settings. Some companies reduce the resultant complexity by relying on a limited set of "pet solutions." If you have only a few tools in your toolbox, it is difficult to respond skillfully when new challenges present themselves. The firm that limits itself to a handful of "off-the-shelf" approaches is deprived of a potentially rich source of innovativeness in its operations. By contrast, the most sophisticated firms experiment in order to discover the most appropriate business models and market recipes for success in diverse foreign environments.

The cultural and physical heritage of the long-established firm gives rise to an organizational culture that frames the context of strategic decision-making. Even as management attempts to adapt to changing environmental conditions, systems, procedures, and processes remain relatively unchanged over time. This inertia limits flexibility as well as the speed and direction of desired strategic changes. Past practices, trends, and strategies within an organization develop a momentum of their own (Collis, 1991). Administrative heritage can lead large, long-established MNEs to undertake international activities that may not optimize organizational effectiveness. Like the Queen Mary, which requires considerable resources and time to execute a course change, large MNEs are relatively cumbersome in the pursuit of new international business opportunities.

By contrast, newer businesses are unburdened by the momentum of administrative heritage. Compared to long-established domestic firms, born globals have fewer infrastructural and mental barriers to overcome in the internationalization process. They have less embedded managerial and physical infrastructure to constrain strategic initiatives. In international activities, youth can confer a higher degree of flexibility and agility, qualities of particular importance in evolving foreign markets. Where the international culture is implanted early, management is likely to be internationally sophisticated and the organization as a whole is likely to be adroit in pursuing and mastering international opportunities (Knight & Cavusgil, 2004). Where internationalization provides competitive advantages, born global firms can often establish such advantages more fully and rapidly due to their lack of rigidities typical of long-established firms.

Organizational learning theory is related to *innovation theory* (e.g., Dosi, 1988; Teece, 1987). According to this perspective, innovation is the pursuit of novel solutions to challenges that confront the firm, including the creation of new products and markets, the attempt to lead rather than follow competitors, and a proclivity for risk taking (e.g., Miller &

Friesen, 1984). As noted previously, internationalization is an innovative act (Simmonds & Smith, 1968). One of the most accepted explanations of internationalization is the "Innovation Model" (e.g., Cavusgil, 1980). Innovation theory is a useful framework because even in the face of limited financial and human resources, early internationalization appears to be a key characteristic of born global firms.

Innovation helps firms respond to changing conditions in their external environment (e.g., Hunt, 2000) and is important for company performance in competitive international markets (e.g., Zahra et al., 2000). Innovation based on technological prowess is a critical entrepreneurial process, particularly in dynamic environments such as those found abroad. Simon (1996) found that his 500 "hidden champions" excelled in innovation and leveraged this capability to succeed in international markets. Born globals appear to be characterized by "innovatory capacity" (Knight & Cavusgil, 2004). Closely related to innovation theory is the concept of entrepreneurial orientation or entrepreneurship. The role of entrepreneurial orientation has gained much credence in research on born global firms and has given rise to the emergence of a new stream of research: international entrepreneurship. Accordingly, we devote much of the next chapter to this important topic.

Orientations and Strategies of Born Global Firms

As we highlighted in the previous section, much research on born global firms has emphasized the roles of resources and organizational capabilities. In this section, we examine the most salient of these. *Learning orientation* involves gathering, interpreting, and disseminating intelligence about foreign markets and alertness to opportunities that exist in these markets. Many born globals leverage "internally focused learning capability," which involves the acquisition, dissemination, and use of information generated inside the firm. It implies an ability to transform internally generated information into knowledge that management can use to achieve international goals (Weerawardena et al., 2007). Such learning engenders innovation and allows the firm to respond to evolving conditions in the marketplace and other external environments (Dosi, 1988; McEvily & Chakravarthy, 2002; Nelson & Winter, 1982). Internally focused learning includes technological learning, which is characteristic of companies that are skilled at adapting to new markets (Autio et al., 2000; Liesch & Knight, 1999). Firms leverage internal learning to develop knowledge that they can apply to addressing external environmental challenges (Autio et al., 2000; McEvily & Chakravarthy, 2002).

"Market focused learning capability" involves the acquisition and dissemination of information from the firm's marketplace (Weerawardena et al., 2007). It involves continuously updating the firm's knowledge base in order to account for new information that is acquired in target markets and the ability to assemble the acquired information as knowledge that management can use to achieve its goals. Closeness to markets and to customers is conducive to rapid internationalization (Knight, 2001) and thus, born globals often focus on their markets in order to acquire, disseminate, and integrate market information to optimize value-adding activities.

Market focused learning capability is closely related to another trait often associated with born global firms—a tendency to focus on markets and customers. Many of these firms develop a complex system of specialized resources that they apply to serve the needs of target markets, resulting in increasing levels of product performance and customer satisfaction. *Customer focus* can be achieved in various ways. For example, the firm may become adept at creating or adapting products to suit closely the needs of specific buyer groups, giving close attention to addressing target market needs via specialized products, using skilled sales personnel and other agents who understand and accommodate exacting requirements, and generally developing strong relationships with buyers. When the firm focuses, it emphasizes depth, instead of breadth, in serving customer needs. In his investigation of 500 "hidden champions," for example, Simon (1996) found that the small, international firms in his study displayed a high degree of focus, specialization, and concentration in serving the needs of their global customer base.

Marketing is the conduit through which companies interact with their target markets, the mainstay of firms' existence. In broad terms, many born globals have superior *marketing capability* (Knight & Cavusgil, 2004; Weerawardena et al., 2007), which represents the firm's capacity to formulate effective marketing strategies. Superior marketing capability emphasizes the skill with which management performs traditional marketing functions such as product development and improvement, product-market communications, pricing, and distribution that direct the flow of goods to buyers located in international markets. For example, Simon's (1996) "hidden champions" revealed a strong marketing orientation. They target international markets via a specialist strategy that focuses on buyer needs using skills for developing and launching distinctive products and services. Superior marketing capability is key to effective targeting of international markets (Knight, 2001) and often implies positioning products in predominantly niche markets (Madsen & Servais, 1997).

Firms leverage marketing to enhance their performance in various ways. The firm can emphasize the "product concept," according to which it offers products and services that offer maximal quality and performance. The firm may seek a close alignment of buyer-seller goals. Where these goals are skillfully aligned, the relative transaction costs for the buyer to seek alternative supply sources are higher. Or the firm may differentiate its products via the development of relatively unique features. This approach can be realized by creating superior products or by undertaking activities that distinguish the firm's offerings from those of competitors. Marketing planning and control, product development and adaptation, as well as skilled manipulation of key tactical elements to offer quality, differentiated offerings, are often critical dimensions.

In a related way, most born globals employ *differentiation strategy*—the offering of distinctive products (Porter, 1980). These firms stimulate customer loyalty by uniquely meeting specific customer needs. There are two main ways to achieve a differentiation strategy: product innovation or intensive marketing management (Miller, 1988). The latter requires substantial advertising or market power, neither of which is typical of young businesses. Therefore, most born globals differentiate via product innovation, often by leveraging new technologies. Private knowledge provides the foundation for new technology development and, therefore, is perhaps the key resource that born globals leverage in order to differentiate products from those of rivals and to overcome the indigenous advantages enjoyed by local firms in the numerous countries that born globals target (Oviatt & McDougall, 1994).

Consistent with differentiation strategy, born globals typically emphasize the development and marketing of relatively *unique products* (e.g., Knight & Cavusgil, 2004). This approach is particularly important for smaller companies that may be unable to compete head-to-head with large rivals. Born globals frequently serve narrow niche markets that may be too small to interest large firms. Marketing scholars have long recognized the inherent value in providing unique offerings (e.g., Phillips, Chang, & Buzzell, 1983; Smith, 1956). The approach is typically associated with innovative product features, excellent customer service, or patented know-how—all factors that distinguish the firm from its competitors (Miller & Friesen, 1984; Porter, 1980). *A priori*, valuable unique products should allow the resource-constrained firm to readily enter foreign markets and may be particularly appropriate to born globals, which tend to hold relatively specialized resources. To the extent the product is unique, a buffer is created against the competitive activities of larger firms by conferring a form of "monopolistic advantage" (Hymer, 1976), and thus aids in achieving company performance goals.

In the course of applying differentiation strategy and offering relatively unique products, born globals often leverage strongly innovative capabilities at the leading technological edge of their industry or product category. Such positioning confers significant advantages for pursuing global markets. Accordingly, *technological leadership* refers to the firm's technological prowess relative to other companies in its industry (Knight & Cavusgil, 2004). It is a type of strategy that many born globals pursue in order to create superior products and improve existing products, as well as facilitate more effective and efficient production processes. For example, the firm may apply advanced production technologies based on microprocessor controls to facilitate small-scale manufacturing that is highly cost effective. Computer-aided design and specialized software allow born globals to produce multiple product prototypes without the need for costly R&D investments. Information-based technologies enable managers to segment buyers into narrow global market niches and efficiently serve specialized needs worldwide. Information and communication technologies help the technological leader interact more effectively with its supply chains and distribution channels. Most born globals that Rennie (1993) surveyed ranked technology as their most critical competitive lever.

Related to technological leadership is the tendency of many born globals to produce *high quality products*. An emphasis on superior product quality reflects efforts to create and market products that meet or exceed customer expectations regarding features and performance. All else being equal, customers favor superior quality products and many are willing to pay higher prices for them. Producers and buyers in global markets environments often benchmark their quality standards against those of foreign-based firms. The new awareness resulting from such comparisons pressures companies to improve. Many born globals emphasize superior quality in order to differentiate goods from those of competitors. Quality has been linked to improved performance in domestic (e.g., Aaker & Jacobson, 1994; Mohr-Jackson, 1998) and international markets (e.g., Szymanski, Bharadwaj, & Varadarajan, 1993). To the extent superior quality reduces rework and service costs while enhancing value, market share and profits can rise and thereby support profitability. For example, born global firms in Australia regard providing quality products as one of the most important ways to international achieve competitive advantage (McKinsey & Co., 1993).

Leveraging quality and technological excellence helps born globals develop offerings that appeal to niche markets around the world. Rennie (1993) found that born globals in Australia thrive by leveraging proprietary technologies and high quality goods. The combined role of global technological leadership, unique product positioning, and quality focus imply that upstream organizational activities related to knowledge development, R&D, innovativeness, and product-based differentiation play a significant role in positioning born globals for international success. While there are numerous approaches for achieving international marketing success, prowess in the development of superior, unique products appears particularly important among born global firms.

Internationalizing firms must choose appropriate entry modes. Given the limited resources of smaller firms, born globals may be unable to undertake costly foreign market entry modes, such as foreign direct investment. Consequently, compared to traditional MNEs, young resource-poor firms tend to favor exporting as their primary entry mode. Exporting offers substantial flexibility for dealing in foreign markets. Flexibility implies the ability to change approaches quickly and cost-effectively, a critical consideration in evolving foreign markets. Accordingly, born globals typically employ exporting as their main internationalization mode, and many exhibit a talent for leveraging the competencies of their foreign distributors. *Leveraging foreign distributor competencies* refers to efforts aimed at maximizing outcomes associated with the activities that foreign distributors perform on behalf of born globals.

The international marketing environment entails unique challenges, uncertainty, and risk, much of which can be overcome by leveraging the localized market knowledge and marketing skills of foreign intermediaries (e.g., Freeman, Edwards, & Schroder, 2006). Distribution partners carry out downstream promotion, pricing, and customer relationship activities. In international markets, strong distribution is perhaps the most important means for carrying out the downstream promotion, pricing, and customer relationship activities of the firm. The born global's relationship with foreign distributors is a key resource because it contributes to the firm's ability to effectively or efficiently provide a market offering to a given customer base.

Industrial networks are characterized by a large number of interconnected firms and individuals who play significant roles in converting resources to products and services for consumption by customers. Several scholars note that born globals typically leverage *networking capability* to facilitate early internationalization and achieve success in foreign markets (e.g., Bell, 1995; Coviello & Munro, 1995; Rasmussen, Madsen, & Evangelista, 2001). Due to resource limitations, born globals are relatively vulnerable to the competitive activities of larger rival firms and other contingencies in the markets where they do business. In order to attain international goals, they often seek to collaborate with partners that have complementary resources (Oviatt & McDougall, 1994; Rasmussen et al., 2001). Network relationships can be instrumental to the discovery of opportunities and the garnering of key resources, as well as acquisition of information that contributes to lowering risk and uncertainty inherent in international markets (e.g., Selnes & Sallis, 2003; Nerkar & Paruchuri, 2005). Network relationships help smaller firms overcome "resource poverty" (Rasmussen et al., 2001). Many born globals leverage the resources of partners for increasing the likelihood of foreign entry success. Collaborative ventures also can provide infusions of capital. For example, Shanghai-based Tri Star International acquired a majority stake in the U.S. firm Adams Pressed Metals, a small manufacturer of parts for tractors and other earth-moving equipment. The partnership provided Adams with needed capital and gave Tri Star access to the U.S. market and marketing know-how (Kaihla, 2005).

A Challenge to Traditional Internationalization Theory?

The emergence of born globals has engendered a degree of tension in the field of international business, partly by highlighting the increasing prevalence of the global start-ups and partly by challenging established theories of internationalization. Two well-known schools of research— the Uppsala Model (Johanson & Vahlne, 1977) and the Innovation Model (Bilkey & Tesar, 1977; Cavusgil, 1980; Reid, 1981)—argue that internationalization is an incremental process, progressing through a series of stages. The Uppsala Model emphasizes incremental internationalization via the acquisition of experiential knowledge about, and gradually increasing commitment to, foreign markets (Johanson & Vahlne, 1977; 1990). According to this view, firms target culturally similar markets and will not commit additional resources until sufficient relevant knowledge is amassed. Because such learning takes time, internationalization is supposed to be a slow process. Then, as knowledge is acquired, resource commitments are said to increase almost ceaselessly, even in the absence of deliberate strategic intent (Johanson & Vahlne, 1977, 1990).

Like the Uppsala Model, the Innovation Model portrays internationalization as proceeding incrementally with the gradual acquisition of relevant knowledge and experience (Bilkey & Tesar, 1977; Cavusgil, 1980; Reid, 1981). The slowness reflects management's inability to quickly acquire relevant knowledge and market information (Cavusgil, 1980). Both the Uppsala and Innovation Models imply that internationalization occurs as a succession of incremental stages. Both approaches are behaviorally oriented and attribute the slow, incremental nature of internationalization to two factors: (1) lack of market knowledge by the firm, especially regarding experiential knowledge; and (2) uncertainty associated with successive decisions to internationalize.

A number of studies have suggested that new ventures can internationalize rapidly after founding in a manner not consistent with the slow process described by the Uppsala School (e.g., Bell, 1995; Knight & Cavusgil, 1996; Madsen & Servais, 1997). Oviatt and McDougall (1994) reported that born global firms often possess an international vision from inception, offering innovative products or services marketed through strong networks, and tightly managed organizations focused on international growth. These scholars were among the first to suggest that traditional internationalization theories may not fully account for the emergence of born global firms. Bell (1995) concluded that traditional internationalization theories do not account for the early international expansion of born globals, and made a call for using the network approach for better explaining the frequently nonlinear foreign development of smaller firms. Knight and Cavusgil (1996) also argued that traditional internationalization theories do not adequately account for born global firms.

For many firms, the first step in internationalization may be one of several other international expansion modes (e.g., Nordstrom, 1991). For example, initial foreign sales may be generated via a joint venture or international network relationships. Companies may undertake foreign licensing, manufacturing, or assembly arrangements directly, without first becoming exporters (Knight & Cavusgil, 2004; Nordstrom, 1991; Reid, 1984). Many firms progress rapidly to direct investment abroad. Born globals show how foreign market expansion can progress very quickly.

While the Uppsala Model's establishment chain assumes that internationalization evolves systematically—from no international involvement, to exporting, to local manufacturing—in reality, born globals may employ a range of entry options, often simultaneously. For example, internationalization modes may include outsourcing, direct sales via the Internet, and complex international joint ventures.

Globalization and the creation of numerous trading blocs have blurred boundaries between "domestic," regional, and global markets. The Uppsala approach does not capture the role of other firm-profile factors such as international entrepreneurship, which has emerged as a key factor driving international market entry (e.g., Oviatt & McDougall, 2005).

Traditional perspectives also suggest that internationalization is often unplanned. However, well-managed firms employ careful strategic planning that accounts for diverse conditions and contingencies in foreign markets. Managers increasingly emphasize planning in international expansion. They account for such factors as company resources, product type, product life cycles, the nature of foreign opportunities, and how to balance domestic and foreign demand. Each decision taken, in the face of numerous variables within and outside the firm, poses differing implications for advancing the internationalization process. As internationalization progresses, often across several distinctive projects simultaneously, the firm adapts to evolving conditions in each venture. No particular foreign expansion mode, once started, is either terminal or irreversible.

Other factors point to a rising tide of early internationalizing firms. In countries characterized by widespread international activities—such as the Netherlands, Singapore, and the United Arab Emirates—there has emerged a "culture of internationalization," in which expertise on international business is more widespread. Technology has played a key role in the emergence of born globals. Technologies such as the Internet connect millions of people across the globe. The dot-com boom of the 1990s led to massive investment in fiber optic telecommunications. Today, the widest range of products and services is marketed online. Transmitting voices, data, and images is essentially costless. Widespread availability of the Internet and e-mail makes company internationalization cost-effective. Search engines, databases, reference guides, and countless government and private support systems assist managers to maximize knowledge and skills for international success (Cavusgil, 2002; Friedman, 2005; Wymbs, 2000).

The Internet has opened the global marketplace to companies that otherwise lack the resources to internationalize. By establishing a presence on the Web, even small firms take the first step in becoming multinational enterprises. Improved availability and quality of information, more efficient data transmission, integration of key markets, rapid improvements and increased investment in various technologies all point to point to an increased ability to internationalize rapidly and target numerous countries simultaneously (Cavusgil, 2002; Friedman, 2005). The emergence in large numbers of born globals represents an important trend, especially when seen in the light of traditional views and frameworks in international business.

CHAPTER 5

A New Field: International Entrepreneurship

Scholars have made much progress toward building a comprehensive explanation on the international expansion of new ventures—one that addresses the initiation, implementation, and effects of internationalization processes in young, entrepreneurial firms. Emergent research is shedding considerable light on the characteristics and performance drivers of born global firms. In the business management field, "entrepreneurship" has long been an important domain for scholarly research. Entrepreneurial activity is critical because it can stimulate general economic development as well as the economic performance of individual firms and might be the key element for gaining competitive advantage and increased profitability (Covin & Slevin, 1991).

For several decades, entrepreneurship researchers have focused on the creation of new corporate ventures and the management of small and medium-sized businesses (e.g., McDougall & Oviatt, 2000). Meanwhile, research in international business long has emphasized large, established multinational firms. This perspective was appropriate because, historically, international commerce was dominated by mature companies that used their considerable resources to configure complex value chains at locations around the world. Indeed, only a couple decades ago, international business was almost completely dominated by large companies like IBM, Sony, Siemens, and General Motors. However, the emergence of born global firms is having a revolutionary effect on traditional perspectives in entrepreneurship and international business. Thanks to globalization, communications technologies, and other facilitating factors, we have reached a point where any company, of any size and resource base, can internationalize early in its existence and successfully ply the waters of global business.

In light of this shift, the born global phenomenon has given impetus to a new academic field: international entrepreneurship (e.g., Giamartino et al., 1993; McDougall & Oviatt, 2000; Zahra & George, 2002). McDougall and Oviatt (2000) define international entrepreneurship as a combination of innovative, proactive, and risk-seeking behavior that crosses national borders and aims to create value in organizations. Other scholars define international entrepreneurship as the process of creatively discovering and exploiting opportunities that lie outside a firm's domestic markets in the pursuit of competitive advantage (Zahra & George, 2002).

In 2004, Oviatt and McDougall (2005) received the *Journal of International Business Studies* Decade Award for their 1994 article "Toward a Theory of International New Ventures." The award recognized the authors' seminal 1994 article, which introduced the phenomenon of born global firms (which they call "international new ventures") to the scholarly audience and integrated literatures from the fields of international business, entrepreneurship, and strategic management. The article also defined and conceptualized "international entrepreneurship" (Oviatt & McDougall, 2005).

International entrepreneurship offers unprecedented opportunities to employ and integrate theoretical approaches that enrich the development of theory and implications regarding born global firms. The new field has gained considerable momentum in recent years. For example, the *Academy of Management Journal* (Volume 43, Number 5, 2000) and other leading academic publications have devoted special issues to this field. Emergence of the field has led to the founding of a new academic journal, the *Journal of International Entrepreneurship*, and the creation of workshops for scholars and students, all dedicated to international entrepreneurship. In light of these developments, international entrepreneurship appears to have attained the status of a recognized field of scholarly inquiry. The emergence of international entrepreneurship is eroding the demarcation between entrepreneurship and international business research.

International entrepreneurship has generated a stream of multidimensional research (e.g., Giamartino et al., 1993; McDougall & Oviatt, 2000; Oviatt & McDougall, 1994, 1997; Rialp, Rialp, & Knight, 2005; Wright & Ricks, 1994). Zahra and George (2002) distinguished two principle streams of research in international entrepreneurship: the growing international role played by young entrepreneurial ventures and the international, entrepreneurial activities of established firms. The first stream emphasizes born global firms. The second stream examines entrepreneurial orientation in the international activities of well-established companies (e.g., Lu & Beamish, 2001; Zahra & George, 2002). It has also been termed "international intrapreneurship" or "corporate entrepreneurship" in international markets (Rialp et al., 2005).

In this way, research in international entrepreneurship often does not focus on born global firms. For example, scholars do not consistently emphasize the size and age of the firm as defining characteristics. International entrepreneurial behavior can occur in old as well as young firms; it can occur in large and small companies alike. Entrepreneurial behavior that occurs in large, established firms is often termed as "corporate entrepreneurship." Moreover, international entrepreneurial behavior can occur at the individual, group, or organizational levels (McDougall & Oviatt, 2000).

In 2005, Oviatt and McDougall refined their earlier definition of international entrepreneurship and devised a model to explain factors that influence the speed of entrepreneurial internationalization. In their revised conceptualization, international entrepreneurship is defined as "the discovery, enactment, evaluation, and exploitation of opportunities—across national borders—to create future goods and services" (Oviatt & McDougall, 2005a, p. 540). This definition emphasizes opportunities available to the firm and permits, but does not require, the formation of new organizations. It also allows for corporate entrepreneurship, which implies that even long established, large firms can engage in international entrepreneurship by creating the appropriate organizational culture, posture, and strategies for proactively pursing international opportunities. Modeling the speed of internationalization begins with an entrepreneurial opportunity and depicts technology as an enabling force and competition as a motivating force (Oviatt & McDougall, 2005a). Internationalization is mediated by perceptions of entrepreneurs inside the firm and the moderating forces of knowledge and networks. The study highlighted the critical roles of technology, competitor firms, organizational knowledge, and networks in explaining the speed and nature of internationalization.

Jones and Coviello (2005) have argued for the development of a unifying direction for international entrepreneurship based on a deep understanding of the commonalities in the scholarly literatures of entrepreneurship and international business. Research on early internationalization can benefit immensely from concepts and ideas imported from the field of entrepreneurship. Jones and Coviello (2005) view entrepreneurship and internationalization are behavioral processes, and develop a general model of entrepreneurial internationalization consisting of two primary process dimensions (time and behavior), and four key constructs (the entrepreneur, the firm, the external environment, and organizational performance). Contemporary internationalization is conceived as a firm-level entrepreneurial behavior manifested by outcomes and events in relation to time (Jones & Coviello, 2005). Indeed, time is a key dimension in research on born global firms.

The Critical Role of Entrepreneurial Orientation

Within the international entrepreneurship paradigm, scholars have examined characteristics that give rise to early internationalization and superior performance in born global firms. One of the most notable characteristics is that born globals tend to exhibit a strong *entrepreneurial orientation* in their international activities (e.g., Knight & Cavusgil, 2004). Specifically, these firms tend to have an organizational culture that supports active exploration and pursuit of international opportunities, with management adopting a relatively aggressive posture abroad. In this way, "international entrepreneurial orientation" represents the firm's overall proactiveness and aggressiveness in the pursuit of international opportunities. It reflects the firm's propensity to engage in "innovative," "proactive," and "risk-seeking" behaviors in order to achieve competitive and strategic objectives.

The innovative dimension refers to the pursuit of creative or novel solutions to challenges confronting the firm, including the development or enhancement of products and services, as well as new administrative techniques and technologies for performing organizational functions (e.g., production, marketing, distribution).

The proactive dimension relates to aggressive posturing relative to competitors, with emphasis on execution and follow-up of tasks in pursuit of the firm's objectives. Broadly speaking, proactive is the opposite of reactive. Born global business activities are proactive, almost by definition, as these firms take the initiative to pursue new opportunities in foreign markets, at or near the firm's inception. Proactive implies being aggressive in the pursuit of opportunities. In their conceptualization of entrepreneurial orientation, Lumpkin and Dess (1996) state that "aggressiveness" reflects a willingness to be unconventional rather than relying on traditional methods of market entry. They cite as examples of such approaches the focusing on specific product categories and "doing things differently" by means of product differentiation (Porter, 1985). Aggressive firms tend to challenge industry leaders, to outspend the industry leader, or to spend aggressively compared to competitors on strategic initiatives (Lumpkin & Dess, 1996).

The risk-seeking dimension of entrepreneurial orientation involves the planning and implementation of projects entailing significant chances of costly failure (e.g., Davis, Morris, & Allen, 1991). Given the complexities of operating in foreign markets, being born global is inherently risky. Venturing into the unknown is a critical component of risk (Lumpkin & Dess, 1996), which appears to characterize born globals well.

Entrepreneurial orientation is a fundamental posture, potentially applicable to any firm and instrumental to strategic innovation (Covin & Slevin, 1991; Miles & Snow, 1978; Miller & Friesen, 1984). Studies have found a positive correlation between entrepreneurship and expansion of strategic activities (Davis et al., 1991; Miller & Friesen, 1984), and between entrepreneurship and corporate performance (Covin & Slevin, 1991; Miller & Friesen, 1984; Snow & Hrebiniak, 1980). Lumpkin and Dess (1996) term "new entry," which is the central idea underlying the concept of entrepreneurship. It is associated with "processes, practices, and decision-making activities" associated with successful entry into new markets (Lumpkin & Dess, 1996). For born global firms, it implies the entering of international markets with new or established goods. A posture that is innovative, proactive, and risk-oriented may be necessary among a class of firms that, in the face of relatively limited resources, takes the initiative to pursue new opportunities in complex markets, typically fraught with uncertainty and risk.

Complex or rapidly changing business environments are best addressed by skillful strategy-making that emanates from having an entrepreneurial posture (e.g., Davis et al., 1991; Miller & Friesen, 1984). Davis et al. (1991) found a positive correlation between environmental turbulence, entrepreneurship, and expansion of strategic activities in the firm. In very turbulent times, experienced managers argue for introducing higher levels of entrepreneurship into the firm's product-market activities and seek to adjust to emerging environmental trends by innovating and updating strategies. For example, as the environment becomes more uncertain, many firms become more market-oriented. As the environment becomes more competitive, many managers focus on anticipating and quickly responding to competitor actions (Davis et al., 1991; Miller & Friesen, 1984).

Companies need both order and diversity in strategy for their ongoing viability. While structure and planning provide order, it is entrepreneurial activity that provides the required diversity. Management at entrepreneurial firms may be more inclined than others to create and activate strategies and tactical maneuvers with a view to maintaining or improving performance. In companies with an entrepreneurial orientation, expansion of existing business, and diversification through internal development, are the means through which proactive opportunity-seeking and problem-solving behaviors are fulfilled. Entrepreneurial activity provides the means to extend the frontiers of corporate capabilities and surpass competitors. The entrepreneur continually searches for new opportunities and problems, and initiates improvement projects to deal with these (Knight & Cavusgil, 2004).

For internationalizing firms, entrepreneurial orientation implies having a strong managerial vision and a proactive posture in the pursuit of international opportunities. Young firms are usually quite susceptible to failure and aggressive posturing is often critical to their survival and success, particularly in new markets. Young companies are typically unknown in foreign markets. They experience a "liability of newness" and therefore must take steps to establish their legitimacy to customers, intermediaries, and competitors (Lumpkin & Dess, 1996). An entrepreneurial posture helps firms to better formulate and realize strategic initiatives that augment their performance abroad (e.g., Lumpkin & Dess, 1996; McDougall & Oviatt, 2000).

Entrepreneurial orientation implies that firms make the leap into international markets because of unique entrepreneurial capacities and outlook. Some emergent companies possess a distinctive entrepreneurial orientation that, when combined with other resources and capabilities such as strong marketing skills, allows them to see and exploit opportunities in foreign markets. While unbridled risk-seeking may engender inferior performance, having an entrepreneurial orientation in challenging foreign environments tends to support the realization of key strategic initiatives that augment international success. Accordingly, international entrepreneurial orientation should be instrumental to the development and enactment of key international strategies in born global firms.

Madsen and Servais (1997) investigated born globals in Europe and concluded that their founders tend to have a strong entrepreneurial sense. Such an orientation is particularly useful to resource-poor internationalizing firms because global expansion implies pioneering efforts within risky environments that are potentially costly, involving substantial uncertainty and hardships. International entrepreneurial orientation may be especially important to born globals because it can drive them to develop high quality goods that are distinctive and technologically advanced, which gives rise, in turn, to born global international success. While international entrepreneurial orientation can probably benefit any firm, the international market-seeking, innovativeness, proactiveness, and risk-seeking associated with this organizational culture appear to be especially salient to born globals.

CHAPTER 6

Implications for Managers: Successful Born Global Firms

Small multinational enterprises now comprise a substantial proportion of new enterprises in Europe, Asia, North America, and elsewhere. Their emergence reflects the internationalization of a class of firms that, until now, were not generally regarded as significant international players. The twin trends of globalization and advancing technologies have contributed to the rise of an extraordinary enterprise that is highly active in international business from its earliest days. Born globals are typically guided by managers who view the world as their marketplace and undertake substantial internationalization from or near the firm's founding. Compared to traditional MNEs, born globals are young—most were founded during the modern era of international trade. Given their youth and paucity of experience, born globals' base of financial and human resources are relatively limited. Nevertheless, many internationalize at or near the firm's founding into a myriad of foreign markets and pursue such targets with entrepreneurial drive.

In contrast to larger firms that leverage economies of scale, big market power, and substantial resources, born globals overcome various obstacles to succeed in foreign markets. Youth and smaller size confer a degree of flexibility and agility that help born globals succeed in foreign markets. Their flexibility is characteristic of young businesses that lack the administrative heritage of large, older competitors. The absence of a firmly embedded infrastructure and managerial mind-sets facilitates early and rapid internationalization.

Born globals appear to leverage a particular collection of orientations and strategies to overcome the disadvantages of being relatively small players in a risky global marketplace. These factors typically comprise a collection of unique organizational resources and capabilities that are especially characteristic of born global firms. The distinctiveness of these resources, particularly compared to better endowed rivals, appears to provide the basis for competitive advantages that contribute to early internationalization and ultimate international success among younger, smaller firms that, in earlier times, usually did not venture abroad. These factors hold special relevance to the success of newly established, highly international firms that today are emerging in sizeable numbers worldwide.

Compared to large MNEs, the importance of "intangible resourcefulness," that is, the ability to do more with less, is relatively important to born global firms. These firms appear adept at leveraging unique and often scarce organizational resources. They manifest specific resources comprising orientations and competencies that are instrumental to the conception and implementation of activities in international markets (Knight & Cavusgil, 2004; McDougal, Shane, & Oviatt, 1994). Much of these resources consist of the know-how, skills, and overall capabilities that reside in the managers who work at these firms. In most cases, born globals acquire learning and knowledge in conjunction with early, substantial internationalization. Managers tend to hold tacit knowledge about global opportunities and the capability to leverage such knowledge in ways not matched by competitors (Mitchell, Smith, Seawright, & Morse, 2000; Zahra, Ireland, & Hitt, 2000).

Born global success depends on developing and skillfully leveraging superior organizational capabilities. The task of management is to determine how best to improve and exploit its capabilities, and to develop new capabilities when needed (Day, 1994). The firm acquires as many capabilities as needed to move its products and services through the value chain. Some of these capabilities must be developed and leveraged especially well to outperform competitors and achieve sustainable international performance. They must be distinctive and allow the firm to attain and support a particular market position. They must be managed with special care through the focused commitment of organizational resources, dedicated individuals, and continued efforts to learn (Day, 1994). Major strategies and other approaches that characterize successful born globals are highlighted in Exhibit 6.1.

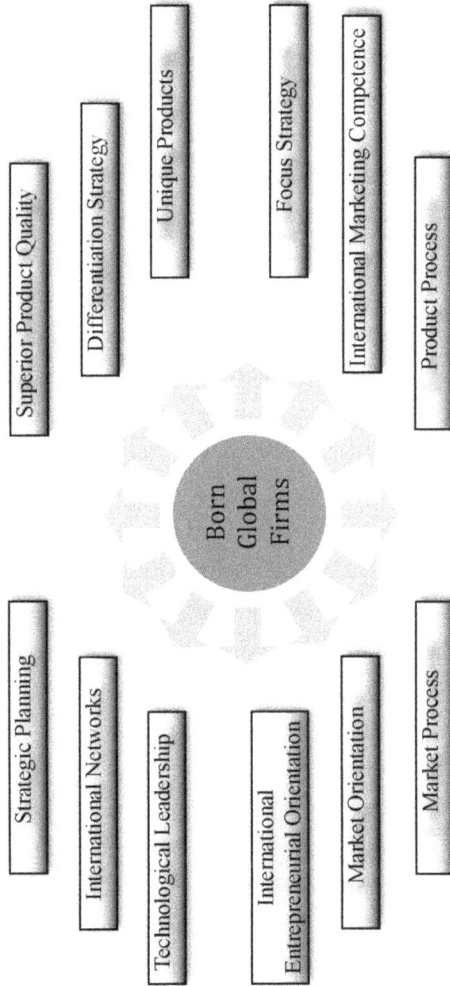

Exhibit 6.1. Strategies and Other Approaches of Successful Born Global Firms

One way to describe the capabilities specific to born global firms is to classify them into two major categories, which we term the "product process" and the "market process." The product process begins with technological knowledge, an important basis for developing and improving products in born global firms. In many cases, technological knowledge intensity in these firms gives rise to an emphasis on product quality, product uniqueness, or both. Born globals rely on technological knowledge in order to develop competitive advantages, which help them project their business activities into world markets. Technological knowledge engenders innovation and allows the firm to respond to evolving conditions in its external environment. Firms that emphasize technological knowledge are likely to develop learning skills useful for adaptation and successful growth in new markets (Autio et al., 2000; Liesch & Knight, 1999). Advances in design and production technologies allow many born globals to perform well in their international activities. In the McKinsey (1993) study of nearly 200 Australian born globals, technology and innovation were ranked as critically important to international success. Possession of substantial knowledge is associated with faster international growth.

As noted earlier, born globals tend to create relatively distinctive products. The McKinsey (1993) study firms owed much of their early international success to the development of relatively unique products. Product development activities are supported by having superior, relatively unique knowledge. Knowledge that engenders technological leadership is often pivotal because it allows born globals to develop distinctive products, differentiate their offerings, adapt them to varying environmental conditions, and achieve faster new market introductions. The breadth and depth of technological knowledge in born global firms is positively associated with international performance (Zahra et al., 2000). Technological prowess gives rise to innovation, which is important for effective firm performance in competitive global markets. Leveraging technological excellence helps born globals to develop offerings that appeal to niche markets around the world.

Having unique products is important for smaller companies that may be unable to compete head-to-head with larger MNEs. Unique product positioning is akin to differentiation strategy and involves creating customer loyalty by meeting the needs of specific customer groups. It is usually associated with offering products that have innovative features or incorporate superior patented know-how, factors that distinguish the firm from its competitors. Prowess in the development of superior products appears particularly important among born global firms. To the extent the product is relatively unique, a sort of buffer is created against the competitive activities of larger firms by conferring monopolistic advantages.

The "market process" implies that many born globals also leverage superior marketing-related capabilities. Market orientation and general marketing competence are often vital to their international performance. Marketing activities tend to follow in the wake of product development, especially in the early days after establishing the firm. Market process activities support early internationalization, but their role appears to be especially vital in the firm's ongoing international performance. "International market orientation" describes a strategic posturing that creates superior value for buyers and, thus, continuous superior performance for the business, in international markets. A market orientation helps management to better satisfy customer needs and minimize rival threats, thereby engendering superior performance. It is comprised of three major activities: (1) being generally attuned to, and collecting information on, the firm's markets; (2) disseminating such information throughout the organization; and (3) creating products, innovations, and marketing activities that are consistent with this information (e.g., Kohli & Jaworski, 1990; Narver & Slater, 1990). Stated differently, the firm implements a market orientation by conducting research to understand market characteristics and buyer needs, by disseminating the research findings throughout the firm, and then by responding to the findings by creating products and services that specifically address buyer needs and wants.

Having a *market orientation* is associated with superior organizational performance (e.g., Dalgic, 1994; Narver & Slater, 1990). Market orientation is an important determinant of success in smaller companies because it may provide a framework for objectives, decisions, and actions (Pelham & Wilson, 1995). In international markets, because the firm encounters a multiplicity of diverse buyer needs and tastes as well as multifaceted competitive threats, a market orientation may be especially important in the performance of born globals. The primary challenge facing born globals is to create value in their foreign markets as efficiently as possible while evading offensive competitor moves. Having a market orientation means the firm attempts to ascertain the needs and wants of potential buyers and then creates products and services that specifically fit those needs and wants.

When they operate in numerous foreign countries, born globals are exposed to a wide range of market environments that form the basis for organizational learning in the context of diverse buyer needs, unique marketing requirements, and tough competitive challenges. Knowledge and experience gained from operating in these varied settings can engender product and process innovations that benefit various aspects of the firm's activities worldwide. The diversity of international business environments enhances the firm's knowledge stock through learning based on interactions within local knowledge contexts and conditions that encourage innovation in the firm's offerings and practices. The diversity of the global environment also offers exposure to new and diverse ideas from multiple customer and cultural perspectives.

International marketing competence is also a critical approach in the success of born global firms. It denotes the skill with which management performs traditional marketing functions—communications, pricing, distribution—that direct the flow of products and services to buyers located in foreign markets. It is interlinked with the firm's market orientation because marketing competence is generally regarded to both support and reflect market orientation. The international context poses numerous uncontrollable challenges that may not be present in the home market. The goal of international marketing and the intended result of superior international marketing competence is to earn the firm a profit through the skillful promotion, pricing, and distribution of products targeted to foreign buyers. Strong marketing capabilities facilitate knowledge of customers, marketing planning and control, product development and adaptation, as well as meticulous manipulation of key marketing tactical elements to target foreign customers with quality, differentiated offerings. Marketing strategy and tactics provide the means to achieve superior performance (e.g., Cavusgil & Zou, 1994). Because foreign markets impose a variety of uncontrollable challenges that may not be present in the home market, international marketing competence is often particularly salient to born global success abroad.

Strategies for International Success in Born Global Firms

Despite the immense hurdles that smaller firms face, many born globals are faring quite well in international business. Research evidence suggests that born globals make use of a particular constellation of capabilities that may help them overcome the considerable challenges of being relatively small players in a competitive global marketplace. Resource-constrained firms can ill afford to commit blunders in their international dealings. Possession of a well-defined strategic orientation is critical to company success. Born globals that do not develop any particular strategic orientation are at great risk of failure. Such a condition is characteristic of Porter's (1980) "stuck in the middle" category of firms that perform poorly.

Managers must develop and adapt strategies to the specific needs of the firm. No single approach is appropriate to all companies, at all times, in all markets. Strategy development and implementation is costly. In the early stages of transition to new approaches, profits may decline as the firm incurs the costs of revising its resource mix (e.g., Mosakowski, 1993; Porter, 1980). Such shifts can muddle the anticipated positive effect of strategy on performance. In addition, strategy may not lead to higher performance if it is poorly conceived or badly executed. There are numerous types of blunders that companies commit in the formulation and activation of strategy that may actually cause performance to decline. In the post-strategy implementation phase, failure to exercise strategic control can also harm financial results. That is, management must take steps to ensure that company goals and objectives are being achieved as per plan.

We delineate specific strategies and other approaches that born globals can apply to succeed in the global marketplace. In general, born globals are entrepreneurial firms that emphasize innovativeness, aggressiveness, and a proclivity for risk-taking. They deploy unique products, characteristic of differentiation strategy. Successful born globals are also characterized by technological leadership and an emphasis on offering products of superior quality and design. Given their smaller size, most born globals focus on niche markets, with many using a focus strategy. Most born globals leverage the power of network relationships to access the channels and resources they need to perform well in foreign settings.

Finally, young firms enjoy considerable flexibility, which is often needed to adapt quickly to shifting market conditions. We next examine some of these approaches in more detail.

We have emphasized the role of *international entrepreneurial orientation* as an antecedent to international performance in born global firms. Strong entrepreneurial orientation is typically associated with the development of strategies and approaches that support internationalization and business success abroad. The proactive development of business strategies abroad is key to company success. Having an international entrepreneurial orientation may also encourage stronger customer focus, which helps engender superior results. Management that develops human and other resources specific to meeting foreign market needs will perform better in those markets.

Entrepreneurial orientation is also associated with innovativeness. Innovation is the life blood of most successful firms. Companies focus on continuously improving products, services, processes, and administrative techniques within the firm. Innovative processes are needed to develop global products and stay abreast of growing global competitive pressures. Various new ideas about how to improve products emerge from dealing in the extreme conditions often found abroad.

We have also highlighted the role of *focus strategy* (Porter, 1980) in born global success. A strong focus on the customer can drive firms to emphasize performance-enhancing business approaches such as superior product quality and competent marketing. A key rationale for pursuing a focus strategy is that the cost of erecting entry barriers in a niche market are substantially lower than the cost of erecting entry barriers in a mass market (Porter, 1985). Resource-constrained born globals that adopt a focus strategy are likely to perform better than other young or small firms that target broader markets. Born globals should focus their resources on delighting foreign consumers and developing prowess in particular product categories. Companies often regard foreign markets as subordinate to the home market. Some firms view foreign markets as a destination for dumping excess inventory or as attractive only when domestic sales decline. In contrast, by emphasizing focus strategy, the firm works closely with customers and is more inclined to adapt products to suit customer circumstances abroad. When the firm focuses, it concentrates its relatively specialized know-how, marketing skills, and other assets on a given customer group or market segment. Highly focused companies are more likely to thrive in their specialized markets because they avoid competing directly with larger rivals. Born globals often develop specialized knowledge of the needs of the target market and work to improve customer satisfaction. Focus strategy allows the firm to achieve superior performance by serving customers well, reducing costs via effective resource use, or both (Miller, 1988; Porter, 1980).

Focus strategy is often associated with providing distinctive products or services. In this way, and consistent with serving narrow niche markets, many born globals offer *unique products* (e.g., Knight & Cavusgil, 2004). Product uniqueness may be achieved by emphasizing patented know-how, innovative product features, or excellent customer service, all intended to distinguish the firm's offerings from those of competitors. Many born globals offer state-of-the-art products that are better designed and higher quality than competitors' offerings. Providing unique products can give the firm "monopolistic advantage," which supports the firm's performance goals. The ability to offer distinctive products often derives from technological prowess in particular industrial categories.

The born global may acquire *technological leadership* as a means of offering innovative or leading-edge products, or devising highly efficient production processes. In fact, the founding of born globals is often associated with the development of new products or services that visionary managers then launch in world markets. The successful firm applies advanced production technologies, computer-aided design, and specialized software to produce superior products.

Many born globals produce high quality goods, offering products that meet or exceed customer expectations. Emphasizing *superior product quality* provides a means to differentiate offerings from those of competitors. Superior and unique products are in turn associated with *differentiation strategy*, whereby the firm targets distinctive products to its target markets. Differentiation strategy may be especially appropriate for born globals that hold specialized resources and operate in niche markets. Growing demand for specialized products has fueled the emergence of countless opportunities for small firms around the world. Born globals primarily achieve differentiation strategy through product innovation, often by leveraging technological prowess.

Focus and differentiation strategies are two of the three generic strategies specified by Porter (1980). The third generic strategy is cost leadership. In our research, we have found that "cost leadership" is usually a poor strategy for born global firms (e.g., Knight & Cavusgil, 2005). This is particularly true if cost leadership is the firm's primary strategic approach. Companies that compete on the basis of low costs alone are subject to severe price competition that puts pressure on profit margins. Such firms are typically less profitable and vulnerable to competitor moves that pull customers away (Porter, 1980; Wright, Kroll, Chan, & Hamel, 1991). Given the competitive position of most born global firms—smaller on average and having little or no scale advantages—primary emphasis on a cost leadership strategy is ill-advised. Compared to large MNEs, smaller firms are less able to compete effectively on the basis of cost or volume. Consequently, born globals should avoid approaches in which cost leadership is the sole source of competitive advantage. By contrast, born globals that emphasize focus and differentiation strategies at the expense of cost leadership or that emphasize other strategies in addition to cost leadership, tend to be better international performers.

Another approach favored by born global firms is the development and leveraging of international network relationships. Developing *international networks* by pursuing collaborative ventures contributes much to international performance. Collaboration makes possible the achievement of projects that exceed the capabilities of the individual enterprise. Collaborative arrangements help born globals achieve strategic objectives, leading to long-term profit maximization (Gleason & Wiggenhorn, 2007). Collaboration helps these companies access "supplementary competences" provided by other, independent firms (Madsen & Servais, 1997). While collaboration can take place at similar or different levels of the value chain, most ventures focus on R&D, production, or marketing. Born globals particularly benefit from partnering with intermediaries that perform a range of marketing functions in foreign markets. They draw on partners' capabilities to market and distribute their products abroad.

How do born global managers decide whether to enter a collaborative venture? How do they decide about the nature of the venture? The typical born global enters a collaborative venture when it perceives that a necessary link in its value chain is somehow weak or inadequate. If this is the case, it then chooses a partner that can replace the function of the weak link. In this way, the firm can meet its growth and other strategic objectives faster or more effectively. Most born globals are exporters and, as they seek to enter various foreign markets, seek partnership with distributors located in those markets. Foreign distributors comprise a sort of "relational capital," providing key advantages related not only to downstream marketing activities but also gathering market intelligence, forging linkages with key foreign contacts, deepening relations within extant markets, and cultivating new buyer segments. Such arrangements also help the firm access numerous markets, as well as reduce the costs and risks of internationalization, access intellectual property and other assets, create synergies for innovative activities, placate government authorities, access protected markets, and prevent or reduce competition.

Another advantage provided by leveraging relationships with foreign partners is *flexibility*. The degree of control in international distribution—the ability to influence systems, methods, and decisions in the foreign market—has a critical impact on the firm's future performance abroad. However, there exists a trade-off between the amount of control obtained and the cost to the firm of obtaining it. Essentially, the greater the control the firm seeks in the foreign market, the more direct responsibility it will have for performing marketing and other functions. In turn, the more of this direct responsibility the firm acquires, the greater its risk will be. But smaller firms with limited resources should avoid substantial risk, particularly in uncertain foreign environments. Control also necessitates committing internal organizational resources, which drives up operating expenses and overhead. This in turn leads to increasing switching costs and decreasing flexibility for dealing with the market. Resource commitment also increases the firm's exposure: that is, the possibility of losses arising from changing environmental circumstances abroad, such as political risk, fluctuating currency values, and other macroeconomic factors (Anderson & Gatignon, 1986). Accordingly, born global firms often benefit from a high degree of flexibility in their international dealings. Much of this flexibility derives from leveraging low-control entry strategies, such as employing independent intermediaries to orchestrate marketing and other activities in local markets abroad.

International markets are characterized by numerous variables and shifting conditions, most of which are beyond the control of the firm. As a company enters or expands its involvement in target markets, many things can go wrong. MNEs work within an administrative superstructure in which plans and corporate discipline are communicated to a mass of employees, partners, channel members, and the like. In general, owing to the momentum engendered by administrative heritage and the problem of escalating managerial commitment, MNEs are often wedded to particular strategic plans. Large firms are generally less flexible than small, global start-ups. The flexibility and entrepreneurial maneuverability of young born globals are key factors that allow them to overcome shortcomings associated with limited human and financial resources. The ability to change systems and approaches quickly and cost-effectively is a critical consideration in evolving foreign markets. Flexibility helps managers adjust plans quickly to suit new market realities. In a world where product life cycles are shrinking and buyer tastes change quickly, flexibility can spell the difference between success and failure. Flexibility gives born globals competitive advantages over large MNEs, which are usually more bureaucratic and cumbersome. This helps explain how born globals succeed even in the face of stiff competition abroad.

The Role of Strategic Planning

In their 1997 study, the Organisation for Economic Cooperation and Development (OECD) found that many small and medium-sized enterprises that succeed in international business often do not engage in substantial formal strategic planning (OECD, 1997). The reason seems to be that, as noted earlier, many smaller SMEs need to be inherently flexible in order to succeed. Successful firms often depend on responding quickly to opportunities or to customer requirements. This does not mean that born globals do not have a clear idea of what they want to achieve. Nor does it mean that such firms do not engage in any planning (OECD, 1997). Indeed, the OECD (1997) found that larger SMEs in particular find strategic planning important to their success. This may arise because larger companies require significant planning in relation to managing human resources. Such firms may be obliged to undertake internal planning in order to provide discipline and to communicate their plans to employees, partners, and the like. In a similar way, it is likely that born globals need to engage in strategic planning as their operations become more complex, with more employees and partners to account for.

Developing an international business plan helps to develop the broad understanding and consensus needed among the firm's managers on conditions in foreign countries, as well as company goals, capabilities, and constraints. The plan helps management account for important facts and objectives, set time schedules for implementation, and mark milestones so the degree of venture success can be measured. It is useful to obtain commitment to the plan from all personnel involved in the internationalization process, as they are the ones who will implement it. In this way, the plan helps to motivate key personnel.

Planning forces management to ask serious questions and think about the future direction of each new venture. Planning often reveals information that encourages managers to update incorrect assumptions. In the course of planning, managers become aware of challenges, risks, and potentially insurmountable problems and can therefore make sound decisions and develop appropriate strategies and tactics. Planning helps to identify and describe problems and challenges facing the firm. Planning can help the firm identify target markets and market segments more skillfully, position products relative to competitors, and devise other strategic and tactical actions that translate into success in target countries. Planning also aids management to think seriously about each current and potential competitor. In this way, management can more successfully develop offerings and approaches that differentiate the firm in foreign markets. In order to aid managers at born global firms in the international planning process, we provide an outline for an international business plan in appendix B.

Other Strategic Concerns for Born Global Firms

As they advance into more foreign markets and gain international experience, most born globals advance to other entry strategies, such as joint ventures and foreign direct investment. Exporting is the approach favored by born globals in the early stages of internationalization. However, exporting has some drawbacks. First, because exporting does not require the firm to establish a physical presence in the foreign market (in contrast to FDI), management has fewer opportunities to learn about customers, competitors, and other aspects of the market. A lack of direct contact with foreign customers means the exporter may fail to perceive opportunities and threats or may not acquire the knowledge that it needs to succeed in the market in the long term.

Second, compared to other entry strategies, exporting is much more sensitive to tariff and other trade barriers, as well as fluctuations in exchange rates. Foreign customers who pay for products priced in the exporter's home-country currency are disadvantaged. When the home currency strengthens relative to the currencies of foreign buyers, exporters are likely to suffer. This results because the cost of exports becomes expensive to foreign buyers. Exporters run the risk of being priced out of foreign markets if shifting exchange rates make the exported product too costly to foreign buyers.

To small companies, swings in world currency markets can make or break the firm. The problem is especially acute when the born global quotes its prices in the customer's currency. Customers prefer to pay in their own currency, and so many born globals feel pressure to use local-currency pricing. But trouble arises when the foreign currency fluctuates so as to depress profits when converted into the born global's home currency.

In order to manage such risk, born globals can use various types of currency management strategies. For example, the firm can purchase "forward contracts" in order to stabilize future home currency-denominated revenues. The goal of hedging is to balance purchases and sales of foreign currencies to minimize exposure to future currency risk. Alternatively, the firm can emphasize efficient company operations, to help ensure survival when exchange rates move in the wrong direction and hurt sales.

Lack of sufficient capital is one of the leading causes of company failure. For many born globals, financing and credit are a problem. Some firms borrow money from banks in their home country or in foreign countries. The loan may be denominated in the home currency or in foreign currencies. However, in addition to potential exchange rate difficulties, borrowing internationally is complicated by differences in banking regulations, poor banking infrastructure, shortage of loanable funds, and problems in the foreign economy. Banks are often reluctant to extend credit to SMEs, so smaller firms can turn to government agencies such as the Export Import (Ex-Im) Bank, a federal agency in the United States for direct loans, working capital loans, and loan guarantees. Financing is available for exports, imports, and international investments.

There are other agencies that serve the needs of small exporters. For instance, the U.S. Small Business Administration helps firms that otherwise might be unable to obtain trade financing. Canada's Export Credits Insurance Corporation, India's Export Credit & Guarantee Corporation, Ltd., and Argentina's Compania Argentina de Seguros de Credito, perform services comparable to those of the Ex-Im Bank. Commercial banks occasionally use government guarantee and insurance programs to reduce the risk associated with loans to exporters. Under such arrangements, the government pledges to repay a loan made by a commercial bank in the event the importer is unable to repay. Similarly, governments in the developing world often provide loans to promote inward foreign direct investment projects such as the construction of dams, power plants, and airports.

CHAPTER 7

Born Globals: The Future of International Trade

Young firms enjoy particular advantages in the internationalization process. Compared to MNEs, born globals are unfettered by bureaucracy, hierarchical thinking, and embedded organizational processes. With a smaller number of employees and less institutionalized structure, young companies are better situated to adapt their systems, routines, and collective employee mind-set to the imperatives of international competition. Born globals are often more innovative and quicker to respond to specialized needs and tastes.

In a world of risk and uncertainty, born globals might be seen as relatively disadvantaged because of their small size and limited resources. According to this view, small businesses lack the massive operations needed to leverage economies of scale across an integrated global marketplace. Skeptics argue that small firms cannot overcome the immense hurdles needed to succeed in a global environment characterized by intense competition from large, better-resourced MNEs.

But this view fails to recognize several factors. First, thanks to advancing technologies, globalization, and other facilitating trends, thousands of born globals are already thriving in countless markets worldwide. Instead of being a burden, globalizing trends are a boon to many such firms. Second, born globals are often at the forefront of new products and technologies that give them monopoly power and unique advantages over rivals. Third, new start-ups' inherent flexibility confers key advantages for adapting to rapidly evolving buyer tastes across myriad markets and industries that larger firms are unwilling or unable to serve. The flexibility afforded through judicious use of foreign distributors enables entrepreneurial firms to respond rapidly to evolving customer needs, competitive threats, and shifts in the global environment.

Finally, the majority of born globals operate in niche markets that often are ignored by larger firms. Such markets allow for sufficient scale economies as well as experience curve effects. More than 50 years ago, Edith Penrose (1959) described how young enterprises exploit the "interstices" created by large companies. Nearly every MNE-dominated industry contains niche markets that hold little interest to large firms. Owing to limits on how quickly they can expand, big companies cannot exploit all emergent business opportunities. The interstices are exploited by new entrants, who gain market niches and, ultimately, distinct sources of competitive advantage.

Born globals most at risk of failure are the less experienced firms, or companies with insufficient resources, or those unable to adapt to the pressures and opportunities of globalization. Unless management can make needed corrections, or access key resources via network connections, such firms are likely to fail. In contrast, internationally experienced born globals that hold needed resources are likely to hold substantial knowledge and advantages. They are more likely to sustain their competitiveness, assume a success-oriented approach to managing the firm, and grow over time. In the long run, some born globals flourish, some founder, and a substantial proportion will merge with large companies. The firms that survive and thrive are typically those that emphasize the strategies and other approaches highlighted in this book.

Youth, lack of experience, scarce financial resources, and limited manpower are no longer significant barriers to internationalization and global success. The traditional model of the large multinational as the dominant organizational form in international business appears to be evolving. Among the firms examined here, youth and lack of experience, as well as paucity of financial, human, and tangible resources, appear to be no longer great barriers to the widespread internationalization and global success of the firm. This outcome is compelling because, realistically, international business is no longer an option for most businesses—it has become a necessity. A purely domestic focus is no longer viable for many companies. Even firms that do not face global competition directly are likely to be affected by international factors; their focus must be broadened to encompass global as well as local parameters. The findings reported here suggest that many new firms are taking up the charge. Based on the trends reported here and elsewhere (e.g., OECD, 1997), it is reasonable to suggest that companies that internationalize substantially at or near their founding will gradually become much more common in international business.

Future Research on Born Global Firms

The rise of born globals poses interesting challenges to earlier views on the internationalization of the firm. Traditional models long have emphasized that internationalization is a slow, almost plodding process (e.g., Cavusgil, 1982; Johanson & Vahlne, 1976). In part, the slowness reflects the view that management is unable to acquire relevant knowledge, experience, and market information rapidly. But born globals seem to be taking an approach that suggests the traditional models need to be reassessed. Small size and limited tangible resources are no longer serious barriers to substantial internationalization and success abroad.

In the scholarly literature on born global firms, much work remains to be done. In many respects, relatively little is known about these firms, how and why they internationalize early, and how they succeed in international business. It is useful to explore here how improvements might be made in future research on born global firms. Consistent with the early phases of research on new phenomena, most born global studies have emphasized exploratory approaches, primarily case studies and interviews with managers in born global firms. Numerous studies have been descriptive, without much emphasis on the development of theory (Rialp, Rialp, & Knight, 2005). Only a minority of studies can be considered to be highly theoretical. Numerous studies have attempted to portray characteristics and behaviors observed in born globals, as well as the factors that determine their performance in international markets. Other studies have adopted more specific research objectives (see Rialp et al., 2005, for details).

Initially, future researchers should aim at unifying and improving the heterogeneous operational definitions that tend to characterize born global research. The development of standard definitions and conceptualizations will help to make future research efforts more understandable and comparable. Diverse conceptual approaches in extant research tend to hinder the development of a generally accepted, comprehensive model of the phenomenon (Rialp et al., 2005). In the future, better formulated and integrated theoretical frameworks will assist in the development of explanations, research propositions, and hypotheses, in both theoretical and empirical works.

Much extant research relies exclusively on a single theoretical framework, such as the Uppsala Internationalization Model or the network theory perspective, to investigate born global firms (Rialp et al., 2005). However, future research would benefit from expanding the base of theoretical perspectives used to explain the phenomenon. For example, future research might leverage the resource-based view of the firm, transaction cost theory, and the organizational capability perspective in order to advance knowledge on born global firms. A case in point is the transactions cost economics view, which argues that environmental uncertainty and volatility should induce firms to rely on relatively flexible entry modes in which the risk of entry is shifted to outsiders (Williamson, 1975, 1985). Overall, transactions costs analysis suggests that, in the relatively volatile circumstances of many foreign markets, or in markets that entail considerable uncertainty owing to managerial inexperience or ignorance, entrants should opt for low-control entry modes. Such modes minimize resource commitments and generally allow the entrant to change partners and other operating procedures quickly, in light of evolving circumstances (Anderson & Gatignon, 1986).

New explanations are needed that examine the strategies that enable contemporary firms to internationalize early. Future research should seek to deepen knowledge about the factors that drive early internationalization. Resultant information would be useful for advancing theory about the different strategies that born globals use to advance their internationalization goals. Integrating existing theories and frameworks provides a more holistic understanding.

Researchers should make better use of extant literature from various domains. Studies should be designed to build on the knowledge generated from earlier research. When results are pooled together across a series of programmatic studies, there is a greater likelihood of producing findings that engender a "synergistic" understanding of the characteristics, theoretical implications, antecedents, and consequences in born global firms. Subsequent work might emphasize further integration of the international business and entrepreneurship literatures. More work is also needed to extend or update the stages models, such as the Uppsala Model (Johanson & Vahlne, 1977), in explaining the internationalization of small firms. Future research can benefit by drawing on theories and perspectives from various domains, including nonbusiness disciplines. Coviello and McAuley (1999) argue that future research should integrate major perspectives, particularly foreign direct investment theory, the stages models of internationalization, and the network perspective. They conclude that born global internationalization can be best understood by integrating major theoretical frameworks.

Numerous past studies were theoretical expositions in which no empirical data was collected. Future research should collect data on born globals in order to gain a realistic understanding of the characteristics and other relevant factors regarding these firms. Scholars should obtain data from various countries, in order to assess the extent and nature of the born global phenomenon in diverse international settings. Drawing data from various settings ensures external validity of findings or uncovers differences in born global firms around the world.

Future research will also benefit from applying both quantitative and qualitative approaches. Longitudinal surveys that employ large-scale samples of representative firms, combined with case studies of both born global and non-born global firms, are particularly useful. Examining non-born globals, that is, companies that do international business using traditional, conventional approaches, provides a basis for comparing and better understanding born global firms. Future research on early internationalization would benefit from a perspective that recognizes that internationalization is a dynamic, time-sensitive process. Accordingly, research designs should allow for investigations that examine internationalization longitudinally. In this way, empirical research would attempt to provide an understanding of how and when a firm's international growth patterns reflect stages, relate to surrounding processes such as networks, or exhibit advanced entry modes, such as foreign direct investment (Coviello & McAuley, 1999).

Coviello and McAuley (1999) identified two pluralistic approaches relevant to investigating born global firms. One involves developing a stepwise stream of research, whereby one study follows and builds on another in a planned and specifically triangulated manner. The second approach is more opportunistic and employs a variety of methods that are integrated simultaneously. For example, researchers might begin by examining company evolution in the context of traditional internationalization models, using interview and survey data to identify, match, and explain patterns of international growth. During this phase, certain behaviors of interest could be identified and examined more fully in the context of other theoretical perspectives, such as network theory. This latter phase might involve obtaining a combination of archival data, in-depth interviews, or surveys involving various network partners. Information gathered at all stages of the research would then be pooled, analyzed, reanalyzed, and updated with further information, when deemed necessary (Coviello & McAuley, 1999). The resultant pool of data would allow for a multimethod (i.e., multidimensional) analysis, thus enabling further understanding of the complexity of the processes associated with born global firms.

Emergent research highlights the role of the entrepreneur in the founding of early internationalizing firms. Managerial vision, international competences, and awareness of growth opportunities abroad allow entrepreneurs to aggressively pursue international opportunities. This perspective contrasts with the traditional view on internationalization, advanced by the stages model, which put the onus of internationalization on the firm itself. The international entrepreneurship perspective shifts the relevant unit of analysis from the firm to the individual manager and gives rise to interesting research questions.

Future research should investigate how orientations and strategies applied by born global firms might be leveraged to advance internationalization and international performance in large, established firms as well. Long established companies can benefit from findings on born global firms by adopting the resources, capabilities, and postures that help the smaller firms succeed internationally.

Scholars should investigate a number of additional research questions:

- What accounts for the early international success of born globals, particularly in light of the resource constraints they typically face?

- Several studies have implied that the age of the firm somehow drives other advantages associated with internationalization. Accordingly, what is the role of the firm's age in the international success of born global firms?
- What specific conditions within the firm give rise to early internationalization? What is the role, for example, of managerial vision and drive, product/process discoveries, and other such factors?
- How do resource-poor born globals reconcile the costly customized product needs of unique foreign markets with the need to achieve economies through product standardization?
- Does early internationalization also occur among firms that specialize in services? If so, how do they differ from early internationalizing manufacturers?
- How and in what circumstances does the behavior of born globals truly differ from larger firms? Research would also benefit from comparative investigations across various levels in regard to company industry, national setting, and organizational resource base (including firm size).
- Are born globals more internationally oriented than other firms that do international business? If so, does this orientation make them more responsive to foreign buyer needs and wants?
- What is the role of network relationships in early and substantial internationalization? How do networks advance early internationalization goals and international performance? What types of network contacts are most beneficial?
- To date, researchers have not examined the longer-term survival of born global firms. Little is known about their survival relative to other types of young companies or other types of organizational forms. Thus, future research should investigate what becomes of born global firms. For example, to what extent do born globals remain as small companies? What proportion become big, successful firms? How many merge with other firms? To what extent do born globals go out of business? How do born globals overcome the "growing pains" of evolving from small to large firms?

Addressing these and numerous other research questions will further elucidate the nature of born global firms. Contemporary scholars of pioneering advantage have discovered that being first to market with a new product frequently poses huge challenges that overwhelm enterprising firms. The expense of being first to market and the risk of committing crucial mistakes are often greater in pioneering firms than in companies that are late-comers to a market (e.g., Kerin, Varadarajan, & Peterson, 1992). Empirical research into this phenomenon is handicapped because firms go out of business before their employees can be interviewed. The tendency to survey only firms that have succeeded as first-movers has tended to bias the results of empirical studies. In a similar way, early internationalization undoubtedly carries important disadvantages. There are likely numerous cases of born globals that failed at internationalization or went bankrupt because they could not overcome the risks of rapid market entry, the challenges of competing against established rivals, or other limitations that encumber young, resource-poor firms. Thus, instead of providing advantages, early internationalization might have opposite effects for survival and growth in many young firms.

Methodologically, much research on born globals is dominated by a positivist perspective. That is, the research is based on modern and logical empiricist traditions in an effort to confirm or disprove identified models and frameworks via testing of purely quantitative data. The disadvantage of relying exclusively on such an approach is that research on the born global phenomenon is still in the early stages. This implies that much more research is needed that emphasizes exploratory methods, such as case studies. Relativist investigations that use qualitative and inductive research hold the ability to provide rich, context-specific description and explanation of born globals.

Often, the best research combines both exploratory and confirmatory approaches, combining both qualitative and quantitative research methods. A methodological strategy based on a number of case-based studies of born globals together with longitudinal surveys of large-scale, representative samples of firms would prove very useful. Research should aim to clarify the performance antecedents, environmental characteristics, internationalization processes, and main characteristics of these firms, as well as the characteristics of the entrepreneurs and managers who run them.

Ideally, research should be pluralistic and "triangulated," employing a variety of data collection methods and analytical techniques to examine various aspects of the phenomenon. Such an approach allows the researcher to combine the most suitable research methods at specific and appropriate stages of research, thereby optimizing the likelihood of generating meaningful knowledge (Coviello & McAuley, 1999).

Once the nature and success factors of born globals are significantly understood, research might investigate which public policy initiatives can facilitate and promote the development and progress of this distinctive breed of enterprise. Current activities of most national export promotion organizations focus on the needs of large companies, as they are structured to support firms' incremental internationalization processes. The earlier and often faster internationalization of born globals presents an important challenge to government export promotion agencies, regarding the nature of support provided and in terms of providing assistance in a timely manner (Bell & McNaughton, 2000). Government agencies should emphasize policies and programs that are tailor-made to addressing firms' specific needs. Public policy should be reconsidered to better address the specific support needs of born global firms. Given the limited financial and tangible resources that usually characterize born globals, public policy might aim at supporting the success of such businesses in their international endeavors. Born globals are often drivers of national economic development and innovativeness. Accordingly, research is needed that assists policy-makers to better understand what types of public policies can best support the emergence and success of these firms.

As they investigate born globals, scholars should employ the most appropriate unit of analysis. Past research on international performance typically has often been conducted at the aggregate level of the firm. Yet the examination of performance and its antecedents at the corporate level has several limitations related to the nature of international business. Many firms pursue multiple foreign ventures and performance tends to differ widely from one project to the next. Given the complexity of the international environment, aggregate measures are frequently inaccurate in assessing performance (e.g., Cavusgil & Zou, 1994). Therefore, when investigating born global firms, it is often best to define the unit of analysis at the level of the firm's primary export venture. In addition, as indicated earlier, future research might also benefit by examining born globals at the level of individual entrepreneurs. For example, what are the particular characteristics of managers best suited to success in running born global firms?

Until fairly recently, international exchange was a relatively resource-intensive undertaking within reach of only the most experienced and resource-endowed firms. However, technological advances and the critical mass of globalizing trends have lowered international transactions costs and tipped the cost-benefit balance in favor of organizations previously confined for the most part to participating in local markets within reach of their limited means. The widespread emergence of born global firms is an exciting trend. These enterprises represent a revolutionary development in the evolution of international business and the future prospects of emergent firms today. As never before, their widespread emergence implies that nearly any company, from or near its founding, can successfully target markets throughout the world. The implications of this trend are important because when an entrepreneurial firm operates abroad during its formative period, it acquires an international identity, a knowledge base, and a degree of agility better suited to pursuing foreign opportunities and generally succeeding abroad.

Other Research Considerations

The defining characteristic of born globals is that they internationalize early. The literature has devised various definitions in terms of their age at first internationalization. Definitions of the period between company founding and initial internationalization have ranged from 2 to 6 years. For example, Rennie (1993) noted that many born globals in Australia began exporting in their first 2 years after founding. However, most scholars appear to use a time span of between 3 and 6 years (e.g., Oviatt & McDougall, 1997). We have defined born globals as firms that obtain at least 25% of their total sales from foreign markets within 3 years of their founding (e.g., Knight & Cavusgil, 1996, 2004).

While there appears to be no standard definition on the timeframe for internationalization, born global scholars should use criteria that are appropriate for their own research, and they should provide substantive justification for this criteria based in extant literature or other strong rationale. The time period to internationalization is important because variations in this gestation period can significantly influence the resources available to the firm. These variations undoubtedly influence the nature of the vision and mission that guide management's strategic choices. Moreover, the use of inconsistent definitions hampers meta-analyses and other attempts to compare results across studies.

Another thorny problem with using age to define born globals is that some new ventures are spun off by existing companies and then benefit from the substantial resources of their parent firms, including their networks and brand names. The potential insufficiency of using age alone to define born globals has led Oviatt and McDougall (2005) to redefine "international new ventures" to focus more on the entrepreneurial qualities of firms. The nature of a company's capabilities and how it competes once it has entered foreign markets might be the most decisive factors in determining ultimate company performance.

Future researchers should note that the nature of born globals tends to differ from country to country. For example, countries with small national markets tend to have a higher proportion of born globals. In some countries, the firms receive significant support from the national government. In other countries, born globals are concentrated in the high-technology sector. A study in Denmark found that born globals there tend to be smaller than such firms in the United States (Knight, Madsen, & Servais, 2004). Danish born globals generate a much larger proportion of their total sales from abroad, compared to American firms. This undoubtedly reflects the small size of the Danish domestic market and Denmark's greater connectedness to numerous countries in Europe.

Several scholars note that born globals are mainly found in high technology industries (cf. Rialp et al., 2005). However, research from around the world suggests that the firms can emerge in virtually any industry (e.g., Knight & Cavusgil, 2004; Madsen & Servais, 1997; Moen, 2002; Rennie, 1993). This tendency arises particularly in countries with small national markets (e.g., several European countries), in which firms often look to foreign markets to find and exploit selling and production opportunities. Research that is confined to any one industry or sector may result is findings that lack external validity and cannot be generalized to the larger population of born global firms. Thus, in order to maximize external validity of findings, born global research should examine such companies across all sectors, not just high-technology areas.

APPENDIX A

Case Studies of Born Global Firms

OmniComm, Inc.

A diversified company with 2,700 employees and $300 million in annual sales, OmniComm handles several major products and is growing very quickly in international markets. One leading product is a two-way satellite message and position reporting system targeted to the military and the trucking and fishing industries. The product was targeted early to Europe, which became OmniComm's first major foreign market. The firm has been serving 16 countries there. OmniComm is also very active in Asia. The firm's founders were technologically oriented entrepreneurs who, from the beginning, made little distinction between domestic and international markets. The satellite reporting system succeeds around the world largely because (1) OmniComm invented the technology; (2) the product is better designed, more cost effective, and of higher quality than those of competitors; (3) the firm specializes in and is highly dedicated to only a few major product categories; and (4) OmniComm enjoys substantial flexibility as a young company. All overseas marketing activities are handled via joint ventures with local intermediaries and other partners. Key internationalization triggers and facilitating factors in OmniComm's success included (1) strong demand for the product in numerous countries worldwide, (2) strongly monopoly position in its products, and (3) heavy reliance on advanced technologies.

Note: Company names are disguised to protect privacy.

AntiTox Corporation

The firm is a dominant player in the manufacture and marketing of products to control toxins and improve quality for the agriculture, pharmacological, and environmental industries. Growth in international sales was strong since company founding and increased at an estimated 10% to 50% percent per year. The firm has a strong technological orientation with great emphasis on product quality. For example, the products are tailored to individual customer needs and all are currently manufactured by hand. Customers buy the product primarily because it has proven effective in detecting harmful toxins and tests can be conducted quickly and cheaply. The product is distributed through strong local distributors in each country who typically handle complementary products. International success is largely attributable to (1) offering high-technology, superior quality products; (2) strong product demand abroad; (3) export push—that is, management is strongly committed to succeeding in foreign markets; (4) significant relationships with foreign partners and contacts in the firm's global network; (5) product-market conditions requiring international presence, that is, demand for the product in the home market is somewhat limited; and (6) the flexibility of being a young, small firm.

Instrument Specialists, Inc.

The founder of this firm invented numerous superior tools and techniques for performing arthroscopic surgery on people's knees and other joints. The firm currently generates about 35% of its sales from international sources. Instrument Specialists has a very strong technological orientation (with at least 15 patents) and is well known among orthopedic surgeons for the innovativeness and quality of its products around the world. Success derives largely from developing and maintaining relationships with an extensive network of physicians, hospitals, and distributing agents throughout much of the developed world. The firm became "international by default" owing to the founder's extensive contacts among physicians in Europe. Instrument Specialists distributes its products via 22 distributors in most of the major countries of Europe and elsewhere. Distributors tend to be small, industry insiders handling a variety of medical products to doctors and hospitals. The firm's international success derives primarily from (1) offering high quality, highly regarded tools and techniques; (2) substantial demand for the product abroad (when it comes to health care, people typically want the best); (3) the firm's extensive international network; (4) the firm's reputation as the forerunner in the latest instrumentation for orthopedic surgery; and (5) flexibility of being a small firm.

Heartsafe Corporation

Having around 300 employees, the firm is a leading manufacturer of disposable medical products used in open heart surgery, with about 25% of sales in foreign markets, where it ventured in its first year of business. The founders were a medical technology engineer and a marketing specialist. The main export markets are Europe and Japan. One founder spent much of the firm's early years traveling to Europe and Asia, doggedly developing markets. In an interview, he stated, "We were always open to getting sales, anywhere." Much of the international success hinges on universality of heart disease and customer demand for top quality. Heartsafe generally sells a standardized product worldwide but makes some adjustments to suit, for example, the smaller physique of customers in Japan. The firm has succeeded mainly through (1) a strong focus strategy ("we treat our international customers as well as our domestic ones"), (2) strong demand for the product abroad, and (3) aggressive promotion of the product in foreign markets.

GeoQuest, Inc.

A small company (only 30 employees) founded by a young engineer that gained considerable popularity with foreign buyers. GeoQuest developed and operates a sinkhole and structural detection system for use in roadway design and maintenance. The system won major awards for product design and innovation. Early in its existence, GeoQuest was enlisted by an international agency and a European government to apply its technology to the detection of land mines. There are some 100 million land mines buried throughout the world in nations such as Kuwait, Cambodia, and Afghanistan. National governments and international agencies have sought to remove them. Current approaches for detecting land mines are dangerous and typically involve soldiers methodically poking the ground with sticks. Thus, there has been substantial demand for a safe, high-tech method. Key reasons for GeoQuest's international success include (1) having a near monopoly in a product that provides a high-tech, greatly superior solution to an important, worldwide problem; (2) strong demand for the product worldwide; (3) management's strong international entrepreneurial orientation; (4) superior quality of GeoQuest's products; (5) strong technological orientation of the firm; and (6) possession of significant global network relationships.

NETSALES, Inc.

The firm's main business is national auctions of second-hand cars by linking buyers and sellers through its patented communications network on the Internet. NETSALES has enjoyed rapid growth and typically auctions hundreds of thousands of cars every year. The firm employs a large team of inspectors who evaluate each car, generating a complete written and photographic description. Car dealers register for NETSALES' service and online auctions are held weekly. NETSALES began selling internationally within a few years of its founding, when it was approached by several global auto manufacturers, including Daimler, Mitsubishi, and Volvo, all searching for an innovative way to boost sales. International success factors include (1) strong international demand, (2) management's strong international entrepreneurial orientation, (3) heavy reliance on advanced technologies, and (4) significant global network relationships.

Netcomm, Inc.

The firm's main business is the development and sale of hardware and software for use with computer network communications and data transfer systems. Netcomm is at the leading edge of numerous firms that serve a substantial market for efficient, global communications. Netcomm's initial success was largely stimulated by the rise of Internet. The firm expanded rapidly, with annual growth rates sometimes in the triple digits. More than

25% of sales come from foreign markets, from bases as widely dispersed as Asia, Australia, Europe, and the Middle East. Much of the international success derives from a solid focus on product development and R&D. To beat the high cost of new product development, Netcomm established a large research facility in Eastern Europe, where wages are relatively low. Other factors in international success include (1) management's strong commitment and international entrepreneurial orientation, (2) emphasis on the creation and marketing of high-tech products for a rapidly evolving international market, (3) strong and growing international demand for Netcomm's products, (4) global network relationships (facilitating new product development and worldwide distribution), (5) strong focus on customers, and (6) heavy reliance on advanced communication technologies for worldwide operations.

APPENDIX B

Developing an International Business Plan

Once the firm has decided to go international, it is useful to develop a strategic plan. The plan helps to develop the broad understanding and consensus needed among top managers on conditions abroad, as well as company goals, objectives, capabilities, and constraints. The plan should account for important facts and goals, set forth time schedules for implementation, and mark milestones so the degree of venture success can be measured. All personnel involved in the internationalization process should agree to the plan, as they are the ones who will implement it. In this way, the plan helps to motivate key personnel.

Take, for example, an international business plan developed to launch one or more of the firm's products in a foreign market. A good international business plan seeks to address questions such as the following:

- Which country or countries should we target for sales development?
- What product(s) do we intend to sell in the foreign market? What modifications, if any, must be made to adapt it for the market? Should we develop any new products for the market?
- What is the basic customer profile in the target market? What marketing and distribution channels should be used to reach these customers?
- What special challenges pertain to the market (e.g., competitors, cultural differences, trade barriers), and what strategies should be used to address them?
- What is the most appropriate price to charge for the product?

Note: This section draws extensively from *A Basic Guide to Exporting*, published by the U.S. Department of Commerce (http://www.usatrade.gov).

- What specific operational steps must be taken in order to enter and succeed in the market?
- What is the timeframe for implementing each element of the plan?
- What personnel and company resources are required for achieving the objectives specified in the plan?
- What will be the cost in time and money for each element?
- How will results be evaluated and used to modify the plan?

The first time that the international business plan is developed, it is usually best to keep it simple, perhaps only a few pages long. This is because important market data and planning elements may not yet be available. The initial planning effort itself gradually generates more information and insight. As the planner learns more about the international venture and the firm's competitive position, the plan will become more detailed and complete. From the start, the plan should be viewed and written as a management tool, not a static document. Objectives in the plan should be compared with actual results to measure the success of different strategies. Management should not hesitate to modify the plan and make it more specific as new information and experience are obtained.

Sample Outline for an International Business Plan

Table of Contents

Executive Summary (one or two pages maximum)

Introduction: Why Our Firm Should Undertake This Venture

Part I—International Business Policy Commitment Statement

Part II—Situation/Background Analysis

      Product or Service

      Operations

      Personnel and Export Organization

      Resources of the Firm

      Industry Structure, Competition, and Demand

Part III—Marketing Component

>Identifying, Evaluating, and Selecting Target Markets
>Product Selection and Pricing
>Distribution Methods
>Terms and Conditions
>Internal Organization and Procedures
>Sales Goals: Profit and Loss Forecasts

Part IV—Tactics: Action Steps

>Primary Target Countries
>Secondary Target Countries
>Indirect Marketing Efforts

Part V—Budget

>Pro Forma Financial Statements

Part VI—Implementation Schedule

>Follow-up
>Periodic Operational and Management Review (Measuring Results Against Plan)

Addenda: Background Data on Target Countries and Market

>Basic Market Statistics: Historical and Projected
>Background Facts
>Competitive Environment

References

Aaker, D., & Jacobson, R. (1994, May). The financial information content of perceived quality. *Journal of Marketing Research, 31*, 191–201.

Acedo, F., & Jones, M. (2007). Speed of internationalization and entrepreneurial cognition: Insights and a comparison between international new ventures, exporters and domestic firms. *Journal of World Business, 42*(3), 236–252.

America's little fellows surge ahead. (1993, July 3). *The Economist*, 59–60.

Anderson, E., & Gatignon, H. (1986, Fall). Modes of foreign entry: A transaction cost analysis and propositions. *Journal of International Business Studies, 17*, 1–26.

Aspelund, A., Madsen, T., & Moen, O. (2007). A review of the foundation, international marketing strategies, and performance of international new ventures. *European Journal of Marketing, 41*(11/12), 1423–1448.

Autio, E., Sapienza, H., & Almeida, J. (2000). Effects of age at entry, knowledge intensity, and imitability on international growth. *Academy of Management Journal, 43*(5), 909–924.

Barkema, H., & Vermeulen, F. (1998). International expansion through start-up or acquisition: A learning perspective. *Academy of Management Journal, 41*(1), 7–26.

Barney, J. (1991). Firm resources and sustained competitive advantage. *Journal of Management, 17*(1), 99–120.

Bell, J. (1995). The internationalization of small computer software firms: A further challenge to "stage" theories. *European Journal of Marketing, 29*(8), 60–75.

Bell, J., McNaughton, R., Young, S., & Crick, D. (2003). Towards an integrative model of small firm internationalization. *Journal of International Entrepreneurship, 1*(4), 339–362.

Bilkey, W., & Tesar, G. (1977, Spring/Summer). The export behavior of smaller Wisconsin manufacturing firms. *Journal of International Business Studies, 9*, 93–98.

Bloodgood, J., Sapienza, H., & Almeida, J. (1996, Summer). The internationalization of new high potential ventures: Antecedents and outcomes. *Entrepreneurship Theory and Practice, 20*, 61–76.

Buckley, P., & Casson, M. (1976). *The future of the multinational enterprise*. London: MacMillan.

Cavusgil, S. T. (1980). On the internationalization process of firms. *European Research, 8*(6), 273–281.

Cavusgil, S. T. (1982). Some observations on the relevance of critical variables for internationalization stages. In M. Czinkota (Ed.), *Export management* (pp. 276–286). New York: Praeger.

Cavusgil, S. T. (2002). Extending the reach of e-business. *Marketing Management, 11*(2), 24–29.

Cavusgil, S. T., Knight, G., & Riesenberger, J. (2008). *International business* (1st ed.). Upper Saddle River, NJ: Prentice Hall.

Cavusgil, S. T., & Zou, S. (1994, January). Marketing strategy-performance relationship: An investigation of the empirical link in export market ventures. *Journal of Marketing, 58*, 1–21.

Chang, T., & Grub, P. (1992). Competitive strategies of Taiwanese PC firms in their internationalization process. *Journal of Global Marketing, 6*(3), 5–27.

Chetty, S., & Campbell-Hunt, C. (2004). A strategic approach to internationalization: A traditional versus a "born-global" approach. *Journal of International Marketing, 12*(1), 57–81.

Chuushoo Kigyoo Cho. (1995). *Chuushoo Kigyoo Hakushoo* (White paper on small and medium-size enterprise). In *Okura-sho Insatsu Kyoku*. Tokyo: Treasury Department, Government of Japan.

Cohen, W., & Levinthal, D. (1990). Absorptive capacity: A new perspective on learning and innovation. *Administrative Science Quarterly, 35*, 128–152.

Coleman, A. (2005, October 26). How to be an expert at export. *Financial Times*.

Collis, D. (1991, Summer). A resource-based analysis of global competition. *Strategic Management Journal, 12*, 49–68.

Coviello, N. (2006). The network dynamics of international new ventures. *Journal of International Business Studies, 37*(5), 713–731.

Coviello, N., & Cox, M. (2006). The resource dynamics of international new venture networks. *Journal of International Entrepreneurship, 4*(2–3), 113–132.

Coviello, N., & McAuley, A. (1999). Internationalisation and the smaller firm: A review of contemporary empirical research. *Management International Review, 39*(3), 223–256.

Coviello, N., & Munro, H. (1995). Growing the entrepreneurial firm: Networking for international market development. *European Journal of Marketing, 29*(7), 49–61.

Covin, J., & Slevin, D. (1991, Fall). A conceptual model of entrepreneurship as firm behavior. *Entrepreneurship Theory and Practice, 16*, 7–25.

Dalgic, T. (1994). International marketing and market orientation. In C. Axinn (Ed.), *Advances in international marketing: Export marketing* (Vol. 6). Greenwich, CT: JAI Press.

Davis, D., Morris, M., & Allen, J. (1991). Perceived environmental turbulence and its effect on selected entrepreneurship, marketing, and organizational characteristics in industrial firms. *Journal of the Academy of Marketing Science, 19*(1), 43–51.

Day, G. (1994, October). The capabilities of market-driven organizations. *Journal of Marketing, 58*, 37–52.

The death of distance: A survey of telecommunications. (1995, September 30). *The Economist*, Special Section.

Deshpande, R. (1983, Fall). Paradigms lost: On theory and method in research in marketing. *Journal of Marketing, 47*, 101–110.

Dess, G., Lumpkin, G., & Covin, J. (1997). Entrepreneurial strategy making and firm performance: Tests of contingency and configurational models. *Strategic Management Journal, 18*(1), 2–23.

Di Gregorio, D., Musteen, M., & Thomas, D. (2008). International new ventures: The cross-border nexus of individuals and opportunities. *Journal of World Business, 43*(2), 186–196.

Dosi, G. (1988). Sources, procedures, and microeconomic effects of innovation. *Journal of Economic Literature, 26*(3), 1120–1171.

Eisenhardt, M., & Martin, J. (2000). Dynamic capabilities: What are they? *Strategic Management Journal, 21*(10/11), 1105–1117.

Emmerij, L. (1992). Globalization, regionalization, and world trade. *Columbia Journal of World Business, 27*(2), 6–13.

Etemad, H. (2004, March). Internationalization of small and medium-sized enterprises: A grounded theoretical framework and an overview. *Canadian Journal of Administrative Sciences, 21*, 1–21.

Fan, T., & Phan, P. (2007). International new ventures: Revisiting the influences behind the "born-global" firm. *Journal of International Business Studies, 38*(7), 1113–1131.

Fernhaber, S., McDougall, P., & Oviatt, B. (2007). Exploring the role of industry structure in new venture internationalization. *Entrepreneurship Theory and Practice, 31*(4), 517–542.

Freeman, S., & Cavusgil, S. T. (2007). Toward a typology of commitment states among managers of born global firms: A study of accelerated internationalization. *Journal of International Marketing, 15*(4), 1–40.

Freeman, S., Edwards, R., & Schroder, B. (2006). How smaller born global firms use networks and alliances to overcome constraints to rapid internationalization. *Journal of International Marketing, 14*(3), 33–49.

Friedman, T. (2005). *The world is flat*. New York: Farrar, Straus, & Giroux.

Ganitsky, J. (1989). Strategies for innate and adoptive exporters: Lessons from Israel's case. *International Marketing Review, 6*(5), 50–65.

Garnier, G. (1982). Comparative export behavior of small Canadian firms in the printing and electrical industries. In M. Czinkota & G. Tesar (Eds.), *Export management*. New York: Praeger.

Giamartino, G., McDougall, P., & Bird, B. (1993). International entrepreneurship: The state of the field. *Entrepreneurship Theory and Practice, 18*(1), 37–42.

Gleason, K., & Wiggenhorn, J. (2007). Born globals, the choice of globalization strategy, and the market's perception of performance. *Journal of World Business, 42*(3), 322–331.

Hedlund, G., & Kverneland, A. (1985). Are strategies for foreign markets changing? The case of Swedish investment in Japan. *International Studies of Management and Organization, 15*(2), 41–59.

Helfat, C., & Raubitschek, R. (2000). Product sequencing: Co-evolution of knowledge, capabilities and products. *Strategic Management Journal, 21*(10/11), 961–979.

Hunt, S. (2000). *A general theory of competition*. Thousand Oaks, CA: Sage Publications.

Hymer, S. (1976). *The international operations of national firms*. Cambridge, MA: MIT Press.

Johanson, J., & Vahlne, J. (1977). The internationalization process of the firm—a model of knowledge development and increasing foreign market commitments. *Journal of International Business Studies, 8*(1), 23–32.

Johanson, J., & Vahlne, J. (1990). The mechanism of internationalization. *International Marketing Review, 7*(4), 11–24.

Jones, M., & Coviello, N. (2005). Internationalisation: Conceptualising an entrepreneurial process of behaviour in time. *Journal of International Business Studies, 36*(3), 284–303.

Judy, J. (1998, July 1). Worldwise women. *Small Business News*, 21.

Kaihla, P. (2005, June). Why China wants to scoop up your company. *Business 2.0*, 29–30.

Karra, N., Phillips, N., & Tracey, P. (2008). Building the born global firm: Developing entrepreneurial capabilities for international new venture success. *Long Range Planning, 41*(4), 440–458.

Kerin, R., Varadarajan, P., & Peterson, R. (1992). First-mover advantage: A synthesis, conceptual framework, and research propositions. *Journal of Marketing, 56*(4), 33–52.

Knickerbocker, F. (1973). *Oligopolistic reaction and the multinational enterprise*. Cambridge, MA: Harvard University Press.

Knight, G. (1997). *Emerging paradigm for international marketing: The born global firm*. Unpublished doctoral dissertation, Michigan State University—East Lansing.

Knight, G. (2000). Entrepreneurship and marketing strategy: The SME under globalization. *Journal of International Marketing, 8*(2), 12–32.

Knight, G. (2001). Entrepreneurship and strategy in the international SME. *Journal of International Management, 7*(3), 155–171.

Knight, G. (2007). The new global marketing realities. In B. Keillor (Ed.), *Marketing in the 21st century*. Westport, CT: Praeger.

Knight, G., & Aulakh, P. (1998). A taxonomy, with performance correlates, of born global firms. In S. Cavusgil & H. Tutek (Eds.), *Proceedings of the conference on globalization, the international firm and emerging economies*. Izmir, Turkey.

Knight, G., & Cavusgil, S. T. (1995). The born global firm: Challenge to traditional internationalization theory. In T. Madsen (Ed.), *Proceedings of the third symposium of the Consortium for International Marketing Research*. Odense, Denmark: Odense University.

Knight, G., & Cavusgil, S. T. (1996). The born global firm: A challenge to traditional internationalization theory. In S. Cavusgil & T. Madsen (Eds.), *Advances in international marketing 8*. Greenwich, CT: JAI Press.

Knight, G., & Cavusgil, S. T. (2004). Innovation, organizational capabilities, and the born global firm. *Journal of International Business Studies, 35*(2), 124–141.

Knight, G., & Cavusgil, S. T. (2005). A taxonomy of born global firms. *Management International Review, 45*(3), 15–35.

Knight, G., Madsen, T., & Servais, P. (2004). An inquiry into European and American born global firms. *International Marketing Review, 21*(6), 645–665.

Kohli, A., & Jaworski, B. (1990, April). Market orientation: The construct, research propositions, and managerial implications. *Journal of Marketing, 54*, 1–18.

Kudina, A., Yip, G., & Barkema, H. (2008, Winter). Born global. *Business Strategy Review*, 38–44.

Kuivalainen, O., Sundqvist, S., & Servais, P. (2007). Firms' degree of born-globalness, international entrepreneurial orientation and export performance. *Journal of World Business, 42*(3), 253–267.

Laanti, R., Gabrielsson, M., & Gabrielsson, P. (2007). The globalization strategies of business-to-business born global firms in the wireless technology industry. *Industrial Marketing Management, 36*(8), 1104–1117.

Lado, A., Boyd, N., & Wright, P. (1992). A competency-based model of sustainable competitive advantage: Toward a conceptual integration. *Journal of Management, 18*(1), 77–91.

Liesch, P., & Knight, G. (1999). Information internalization and hurdle rates in SME internationalization. *Journal of International Business Studies, 30*(1), 383–394.

Loane, S. (2006). The role of the internet in the internationalization of small and medium sized companies. *Journal of International Entrepreneurship, 3*, 263–277.

Lu, J., & Beamish, P. (2001). The internationalization and performance of SMEs. *Strategic Management Journal, 22*(6/7), 565–586.

Lumpkin, G., & Dess, G. (1996). Clarifying the entrepreneurial orientation construct and linking it to performance. *Academy of Management Review, 21*(1), 135–172.

Luostarinen, R., & Gabrielsson, M. (2006). Globalization and marketing strategies of born globals in SMOPECs. *Thunderbird International Business Review, 48*(6), 773–801.

Luostarinen, R., Korhonen, H., Jokinen, J., & Pelkonen, T. (1994). *Globalization and SME (59)*. Helsinki, Finland: Ministry of Trade and Industry.

Madsen T., & Servais, P. (1997). The internationalization of born globals: An evolutionary process. *International Business Review, 6*(6), 1–14; 561–583.

Mahoney, J. (1995). The management of resources and the resource of management. *Journal of Business Research, 33*(2), 91–101.

Mathews, J., & Zander, I. (2007). The international entrepreneurial dynamics of accelerated internationalisation. *Journal of International Business Studies, 38*(3), 387–403.

Matlack, C. (2006, October 30). Europe: Go east, young man. *Business Week.*

McDougall, P. (1989). International versus domestic entrepreneurship: New venture strategic behavior and industry structure. *Journal of Business Venturing, 4*(6), 387–400.

McDougall, P., & Oviatt, B. (2000). International entrepreneurship: The intersection of two research paths. *Academy of Management Journal, 43*(5), 902–906.

McDougall, P., Oviatt, B., & Shrader, R. (2003). A comparison of international and domestic new ventures. *Journal of International Entrepreneurship, 1*(1), 59–82.

McDougall, P., Shane, S., & Oviatt, B. (1994). Explaining the formation of international new ventures: The limits of theories from international business research. *Journal of Business Venturing, 9*(6), 469–487.

McEvily, S., & Chakravarthy, B. (2002). The persistence of knowledge-based advantage: An empirical test for product performance and technological knowledge. *Strategic Management Journal, 23*(4), 285–305.

McKinsey & Co. (1993). *Emerging exporters: Australia's high value-added manufacturing exporters*. Melbourne: Australian Manufacturing Council.

McNaughton, R. (2003). The number of export markets that a firm serves: Process models versus the born-global phenomenon. *Journal of International Entrepreneurship, 1*(3), 297–307.

Michailova, S., & Wilson, H. (2008). Small firm internationalization through experiential learning: The moderating role of socialization tactics. *Journal of World Business, 43*(2), 243–254.

Miles, R., & Snow, C. (1978). *Organizational strategy, structure, and process*. New York: McGraw-Hill.

Miller, D. (1988). Relating Porter's business strategies to environment and structure: Analysis and performance implications. *Academy of Management Journal, 31*(2), 280–308.

Miller, D., & Friesen, P. (1984). *Organizations: A quantum view*. Englewood Cliffs, NJ: Prentice-Hall.

Mitchell, R., Smith, B., Seawright, K., & Morse, E. (2000). Cross-cultural cognitions and the venture creation decision. *Academy of Management Journal, 43*(5), 974–993.

Moen, O. (2002). The born globals: A new generation of small European exporters. *International Marketing Review, 19*(2/3), 156–175.

Moen, O., & Servais, P. (2002). Born global or gradual global? Examining the export behavior of small and medium-sized enterprises. *Journal of International Marketing, 10*(3), 49–72.

Mohr-Jackson, I. (1998). Conceptualizing total quality orientation. *European Journal of Marketing, 32*(1/2), 13–22.

Mort, G., & Weerawardena, J. (2006). Networking capability and international entrepreneurship: How networks function in Australian born global firms. *International Marketing Review, 23*(5), 549–572.

Mosakowski, E. (1993). A resource-based perspective on the dynamic strategy-performance relationship: An empirical examination of the focus and differentiation strategies in entrepreneurial firms. *Journal of Management, 19*(4), 819–839.

Mudambi, R., & Zahra, S. (2007). The survival of international new ventures. *Journal of International Business Studies, 38*(2), 333–352.

Nakamura, S. (1992). *21 seiki gata chuushoo kigyoo* (21st century-style small and medium size enterprises). Tokyo: Iwanami Shoten.

Narver, J., & Slater, S. (1990). The effect of a market orientation on business profitability. *Journal of Marketing, 54*(4), 20–35.

Nelson, R., & Winter, S. (1982). *An evolutionary theory of economic change.* Cambridge, MA: Belknap Press.

Nerkar, A., & Paruchuri, S. (2005). Evolution of R&D capabilities: The role of knowledge networks within a firm. *Management Science, 51*(5), 771–786.

Neupert, K., Baughn, C., & Dao, T. (2006). SME exporting challenges in transitional and developed economies. *Journal of Small Business and Enterprise Development, 13*(4), 535–544.

Nikkei Sangyoo Shimbun. (1995). *Benchaa shin sedai* (New generation ventures). Tokyo: Nihon Keizai Shimbun Sha.

Nonaka, I. (1994, February). A dynamic theory of organizational knowledge creation. *Organization Science, 5,* 14–37.

Nordstrom, K. (1991). *The internationalization process of the firm.* Unpublished doctoral dissertation, Institute of International Business, Stockholm School of Economics.

OECD. (1997). *Globalization and small and medium enterprises (SMEs).* Paris: Organization for Economic Co-operation and Development.

Oviatt, B., & McDougall P. (1994). Toward a theory of international new ventures. *Journal of International Business Studies, 25*(1), 45–64.

Oviatt, B., & McDougall, P. (1995). Global start-ups: Entrepreneurs on a worldwide stage. *Academy of Management Executive, 9*(2), 30–43.

Oviatt, B., & McDougall, P. (1997). Challenges for internationalization process theory: The case of international new ventures. *Management International Review, 37*(2), 85–99.

Oviatt, B., & McDougall, P. (2005a). Defining international entrepreneurship and modeling the speed of internationalization. *Entrepreneurship Theory & Practice, 29*(5), 537–553.

Oviatt, B., & McDougall, P. (2005b). The internationalization of entrepreneurship. *Journal of International Business Studies, 36*(1), 2–8.

Pavilkey, S. (2001, January 19). Pet product maker gives international clients royal treatment. *Business First,* p. A20.

Pelham, A., & Wilson, D. (1995). *Does market orientation matter for small firms?* (pp. 95–102). Cambridge, MA: Marketing Science Institute.

Peng, M., & York, A. (2001). Behind intermediary performance in export trade: Transactions, agents, and resources. *Journal of International Business Studies, 32*(2), 327–346.

Phillips, L., Chang, D., & Buzzell, R. (1983, Spring). Product quality, cost position, and business performance: A test of some key hypotheses. *Journal of Marketing, 47,* 26–43.

Porter, M. (1980). *Competitive strategy*. New York: Free Press.

Porter, M. (1985). *Competitive advantage: Creating and sustaining superior performance*. New York: Free Press.

Rahman, B. (1999, July 22). Extra eye on land mines. *Financial Times*.

Rasmussen, E., Madsen, T., & Evangelista, F. (2001). The founding of the born global company in Denmark and Australia: Sensemaking and networking. *Asia Pacific Journal of Marketing and Logistics, 13*(3), 75–107.

Reid, S. (1981, Fall). The decision-maker and export entry and expansion. *Journal of International Business Studies, 12*, 101–11.

Rennie, M. (1993). Born global. *McKinsey Quarterly, 4*, 45–52.

Rialp, A., & Rialp, J. (2006). Faster and more successful exporters: An exploratory study of born global firms from the resource-based view. *Journal of Euro-Marketing, 16*(1/2), 71–86.

Rialp, A., Rialp, J., & Knight, G. (2005). The phenomenon of early internationalizing firms: What do we know after a decade (1993–2003) of scientific inquiry? *International Business Review, 14*(2), 147–166.

Roux, E. (1979). The export behavior of small and medium size French firms. In L. Mattsson & F. Wiedersheim-Paul (Eds.), *Recent research on the internationalization of business*. Uppsala, Sweden: Proceedings of the Annual Meeting of the European International Business Association.

Selnes, F., & Sallis, F. (2003). Promoting relationship learning. *Journal of Marketing, 67*(3), 80–89.

Servais, P., Madsen, T., & Rasmussen, E. (2007). Small manufacturing firms' involvement in international e-business activities. *Advances in International Marketing, 17*, 297–309.

Servais, P., Zucchella, A., & Palamara, G. (2006). International entrepreneurship and sourcing: International value chain of small firms. *Journal of Euromarketing, 16*(1/2), 105–117.

Sharma, D., & Blomstermo, A. (2003). The internationalization process of born globals: A network view. *International Business Review, 12*(6), 657–788.

Simmonds, K., & Smith, H. (1968). The first export order: A marketing innovation. *British Journal of Marketing, 2*(2), 93–100.

Simon, H. (1996). *Hidden champions: Lessons from 500 of the world's best unknown companies*. Boston: Harvard Business School Press.

Small firms aren't waiting to grow up to go global. (1989, December 5). *Wall Street Journal*, p. B2.

Smith, W. (1956, July). Product differentiation and market segmentation as alternative marketing strategies. *Journal of Marketing, 21*, 3–8.

Snow, C., & Hrebiniak, L. (1980, June). Strategy, distinctive competence, and organizational performance. *Administrative Science Quarterly, 25*, 317–336.

Szymanski, D., Bharadwaj, S., & Varadarajan, P. (1993, October). Standardization versus adaptation of international marketing strategy: An empirical investigation. *Journal of Marketing, 57,* 1–17.

Teece, D. (1987). *The competitive challenge: Strategies for industrial innovation and renewal.* Cambridge, MA: Ballinger.

Teece, D., Pisano, G., & Shuen, A. (1997). Dynamic capabilities and strategic management. *Strategic Management Journal, 18,* 509–533.

United Nations. (1993). *Small and medium-sized transnational corporations: Role, impact and policy implications.* New York: United Nations Conference on Trade and Development.

Vernon, R. (1966). International investment and international trade in the product cycle. *Quarterly Journal of Economics, 80,* 190–207.

Weerawardena, J., Mort, G., Liesch, P., & Knight, G. (2007). Conceptualizing accelerated internationalization in the born global firm: A dynamic capabilities perspective. *Journal of World Business, 42*(3), 294–303.

Wernerfelt, B. (1984). A resource-based view of the firm. *Strategic Management Journal, 5*(2), 171–180.

Williamson, O. (1975). *Markets and hierarchies: Analysis and antitrust implications.* New York: Free Press.

Williamson, O. (1985). *The economic institutions of capitalism.* New York: Free Press.

World Bank. (2005). *2004 Annual review: Small business activities.* Washington, DC: World Bank Group.

Wright, P., Kroll, M., Chan, P., & Hamel, K. (1991). Strategic profiles and performance: An empirical test of select key propositions. *Journal of the Academy of Marketing Science, 19*(3), 245–54.

Wright, R., & Ricks, D. (1994). Trends in international business research: Twenty-five years later. *Journal of International Business Studies, 25*(4), 687–701.

Wymbs, C. (2000). How e-commerce is transforming and internationalizing service industries. *Journal of Services Marketing, 14*(6), 463–471.

Yeoh, P. (2000). Information acquisition activities: A study of global start-up exporting companies. *Journal of International Marketing, 8*(3), 36–60.

Yeoh, P. (2004). International learning: Antecedents and performance applications among newly internationalizing companies in an exporting context. *International Marketing Review, 21*(4/5), 511–522.

Zahra, S., & George, G. (2002). International entrepreneurship: The current status of the field and future research agenda. In M. Hitt, R. Ireland, M. Camp, & D. Sexton (Eds.), *Strategic leadership: Creating a new mindset* (pp. 255–288). London: Blackwell.

Zahra, S., Ireland, D., & Hitt, M. (2000). International expansion by new venture firms: International diversity, mode of market entry, technological learning, and performance. *Academy of Management Journal, 43*(5), 925–950.

Zhang, M., & Tansuhaj, P. (2007). Organizational culture, information technology capability, and performance: The case of born global firms. *Multinational Business Review, 15*(3), 43–78.

Zhou, L. (2007). The effects of entrepreneurial proclivity and foreign market knowledge on early internationalization. *Journal of World Business, 42*(3), 281–293.

Zhou, L., Wu, W., & Luo, X. (2007). Internationalization and the performance of born-global SMEs: The mediating role of social networks. *Journal of International Business Studies, 38*(4), 673–690.

Zollo, M., & Winter, S. (2002). Deliberate learning and the evolution of dynamic capabilities. *Organization Science, 13*(3), 339–351.

Index

www.ingramcontent.com/pod-product-compliance
Lightning Source LLC
Chambersburg PA
CBHW062023200326
41519CB00017B/4902